Am I Blue?

Living
with Diabetes
and, Dammit, Having Fun!

ELAINE STRITCH

M. Evans and Company, Inc.
New York

Library of Congress Cataloging in Publication Data

Stritch, Elaine.
  Am I blue?

  Bibliography: p.
  Includes index.
  1. Stritch, Elaine. 2. Diabetes—Patients—United
States—Biography. 3. Diabetes—Patients—Rehabilitation.
I. Title.
RC660.S77   1984   362.1′96462′00924   [B]   84-6041

ISBN 0-87131-428-2

M. Evans and Company, Inc.
216 East 49 Street
New York, New York 10017

Design by James L. McGuire

Manufactured in the United States of America

9 8 7 6 5 4 3 2 1

To my husband, John Bay, who was, incidentally, responsible for the title of this book. I used to jump for joy in the morning when my Clinitest showed blue in the test tube. "I'm blue! I'm blue!" I would shout out from the loo, which meant of course that my blood sugar was more or less normal. One morning John shouted back, "That's it, kid. That's the title—*Am I Blue?*"

John lived by my side—and died by my side. He did both with warmth and love, courage and style, humor and grace. He was the most adorable guy who ever lived.

This book is for John and—I'm sure he wouldn't mind—for you.

Acknowledgments

I am immensely grateful to Peter Evans, science journalist, broadcaster, and author of several books on health matters, for helping me with the medical details in this book.

Thanks are due to the following for permission to reproduce copyright material:

American Diabetes Association, Inc., and The American Dietetic Association for "Food Lists" in Appendix 1.

Becton Dickinson Consumer Products, Rochelle Park, New Jersey, for the photographs of "Drawing Insulin" and "Injecting Insulin."

The British Diabetic Association for extracts from their publications.

The British Medical Association for the table from *Life with Diabetes* by Dr. Arnold Bloom.

W. B. Saunders for "Insulins Currently Available in the United States" from *Clinical Diabetes Mellitus* by George Kozak, M.D.

Contents

Note to the American Edition

Am I Blue? was originally published in Great Britain. Information in the book that is equally appropriate for British and American readers has been left unchanged. Other material (such as the chart of insulins and the reading list) has been adapted for this American edition. There is variation in the treatment of diabetes, however, and readers who have questions about specific recommendations should consult their physicians.

Foreword

Diabetes strikes an estimated 600,000 new people in the United States every year. In 1978 it struck Elaine Stritch, an active, involved, spontaneous actress who was then living in England. She responded in her characteristic "take charge" fashion, deciding to learn as much as possible about her disease, take good care of herself, and have some fun in the process.

There is certainly a great deal to learn, for patient and physician alike. Diabetes affects every organ system in the body, from the eyes to the skin to the feet. As Elaine Stritch mentions in her book, there is an old adage among physicians: "Know syphilis, know medicine." Today that saying is perhaps more appropriately applied to diabetes, with all its physical and psychological ramifications.

This book is an excellent first step toward learning about diabetes, a resource to help you learn about proper diet, exercise, and insulin in order to promote enhanced physical and emotional well-being. As a physician, I have no doubt in my mind that the patients who know the most do the best job of taking care of themselves. More than with any other chronic illness, diabetic patients are in charge of the day-to-day and week-to-week management of their illness. Fortunately, technological advances in home glucose monitoring have made this process easier and much more rewarding, so that more people can establish good control of their diabetes and thereby diminish, it is hoped, the long-term vascular complications.

In addition to serving as an information resource, Elaine Stritch's book reveals an important aspect of dealing with a chronic illness: a positive, optimistic attitude. It is a sensitive statement by a woman who did not become depressed or overwhelmed by the changes demanded by her new life-style, but rather made the changes with good humor, accepted the challenge of control, and in taking an active role in her illness gained a new sense of confidence and well-being, goals that we all share, diabetic and non-diabetic alike.

Doreen Gluckin, M.D.

Overture

When I found out I was diabetic, my first instinct was to tell the world. I guess it's the actress in me. I have always shared my experiences, good or bad, with anybody and everybody who would listen. Now I would like to share my feelings about diabetes with as many diabetics as I possibly can.

Hence my book, *Am I Blue?* Hell, no! Well, in the Clinitest test tube, I hope, yes. In life, I repeat: hell, no!

I have come to know about and have talked to so many diabetics since I "joined the club," and I have found that they are frightened, embarrassed, and shy about their condition. They don't want to talk about it to anybody; they are reluctant to let anybody even know about it.

If you're a diabetic and feel this way, you're nuts! Give me a crack at straightening you out. Turn the pages and read this book. Why not make the most out of whatever your "load to bear" in life happens to be? Maybe I can persuade you that if you're diabetic, you didn't get such a bad shake of the dice after all because, if you take care of yourself and follow the rules, you may still end up a winner.

1

What Is Going On?

I was feeling good—in fact terrific. I'd never been so
happy in my whole life. It was early 1978 and my career
was going full tilt. My successful television series with
Donald Sinden, "Two's Company," was giving me satisfaction and discipline. Behind me was a Royal Command
Performance in front of the Queen at the London Palla-
dium that had been enthusiastically received all around,
and ahead stretched all sorts of interesting projects, offers,
and ambitions. I was, in middle age, blossoming like a girl
on her wedding or first communion day, and bubbling
along with more energy and drive than I could remember
myself mustering in a long time.

Then I was offered a part in a play, a revival of *Fatal
Weakness* in Windsor. To be frank, I didn't much like the
play itself, nor was my part absolutely ideal at first glance.
I was to play a nonsmoking teetotaler, while cigarettes and
alcohol had been two of my chief props for many years. On
the other hand, the challenge appealed to me. I am the
kind of person who will give herself problems deliberately
to prove a point. So why not take the part?

Well, take it I did and settled down to work myself
into the character. And when I say work I mean work, far
beyond the call of duty. I began also to lose weight, which
for me was not uncommon during strenuous periods, so I
simply looked on my *Harper's Bazaar* figure as a bonus that

1

went with the job. On opening night I strode onstage—
and blew my lines all over it. I was terrible. Nothing went
right, and not even the kindness of the critics, who said it
was a poor play anyway and unworthy of my talent, etc.,
etc., could disguise the fact that there was, in the words of
my good friend Marti Stevens, "none of Elaine Stritch in
it." One thing that the critics did not say was that the
leading lady had had a drink or two, which they very well
might have done because that was just the way it must
have looked from where they were sitting. It was not only a
matter of muffing lines. I felt out of control of all my
movements, and much as I tried to cover my inadequacies
I felt afterward deeply shocked at myself for having given
such a performance.

Four weeks later the play closed, during which time I
had improved enormously. But I continued to lose weight,
not to the point where I looked gaunt or odd, yet enough to
bring me down to about 112 pounds, and still falling. As I
drove home from Windsor after the play closed, the memory of that dreadful opening night had receded and I felt a
deep sense of well-being. I was looking forward to a well-
deserved rest from the nightly routines of costumes and
makeup. Then something strange happened. It was a
small thing really, but at the time it inexplicably took on a
terrific significance. Looking out of the car window at the
beautiful Thames Valley scenery, I suddenly felt like whis-
tling. But I couldn't. I blew and blew, but not one solitary
sound came out. "Why can't I whistle?" I asked my
husband, John Bay, and another actor who was driving us
home. "Does it mean," I added jokingly, "that I'll never
be able to do another musical?" They gave me reasons
why I couldn't whistle. I was tired. I still had not wound
down after the play. I was thirsty. "But I've been tired,
strung out, and thirsty before, and I've usually managed
to get out at least one little cheep when I've wanted to," I

retorted. They carried on reassuring me, but I lapsed into silence, brooding over what had become a monumental problem, the case of the disappearing whistle.

Back in London a few days after this, I stood on the scales and saw that my weight was little more than 105 pounds. I was still feeling healthy, though, and once more fully occupied with a new project, this time a radio play for the BBC called—prophetically, as it was to turn out—*A Delicate Balance*, by Edward Albee, whose work I had always admired. Once more into rehearsals every day. Read, study, discuss, rehearse, then record. Hard work, and enjoyable. Of course I felt tired, but so does anyone when under pressure. So there hardly seemed anything to worry about.

Then two recurrent habits began to emerge. Living within walking distance of Broadcasting House, I have always preferred to get there on foot rather than use any other form of transport. But I found myself starting to hail cabs around Liberty's—about ten minutes' walk from the BBC. "That's funny," I thought, "I'm not late or anything, but I am so tired it's ridiculous." Then once in the cab I would suddenly find myself seized with a tremendous thirst. I would get the cabby to pull over to the curb and literally run into a café like Ray Milland in *The Lost Weekend*. But all I wanted was a Coke. And this only fifty yards or so from the BBC! I had to have that Coca-Cola. It was a matter of life and death. Why?

One morning, during a rehearsal for *A Delicate Balance*, the actress Irene Worth, who was in the play with me, suddenly turned to me and said, "Elaine, you don't drink alcohol anymore, do you?"

"No," I answered. "Do I look like I do?"

She laughed but went on to ask me seriously why I drank six Coca-Colas before the 11:30 tea break. Before I could answer, Irene said, "Look, you don't seem well at all, so why not pop along to see a nurse here in the lunch hour, just to have her take your temperature?'' There was something about the concern in her voice that made me do exactly as she suggested.

In the surgery a little French nurse looked at me carefully and said, ''Oh dear, I don't want to alarm you, but I think I ought to take a urine specimen.'' This she did, disappeared for a while, and came out from the other room with an even more peculiar expression on her face. ''I think,'' she said, ''you had better go and see your doctor first thing in the morning because I'm not allowed to take a blood test.'' My God, I thought, what's wrong with me? She saw my alarm and became reassuring. ''There's nothing to get excited about, but I think your blood sugar level is very high.''

''Oh, well,'' I said, somewhat relieved. ''That's understandable because I just drank six Cokes.'' She laughed, but not wholeheartedly; she was genuinely concerned.

The next morning I was at my doctor's office and he confirmed that my blood sugar was high. He prescribed some tablets to see if they would bring about an improvement, while I went on to record the last part of the radio play, grateful that I had been able to get through it without feeling too bad, just extremely tired and of course looking very, very thin. The bathroom scales by this time were giving me a reading of 98 pounds. At the end of those two days, though, I knew before my doctor told me that things were not going to go on like this for much longer. In fact the next day I was—he said—to go into the hospital. London Clinic here I come, all 91 pounds of me. Too bad I didn't feel like going out to some spiffy place to dinner: I looked like a *Vogue* model.

There was not much time to think about things, now that the die was cast, but I do remember weighing myself the night before I went in and again in the morning and finding that, overnight, I had lost no less than 7 pounds. This alone was enough to force me to realize that, whatever diabetes was all about, it could be lethal if left untreated. So the London Clinic looked pretty good from where I was sitting.

I'm a good patient. I have always had a childlike faith in hospitals and doctors, so much so that I often make the Freudian slip of saying to people, "When I was in the *hotel*," when I mean "the hospital." So I put myself completely in medical hands. They gave me an injection of I knew not what (nor cared, simply wanting whatever it was in the hypodermic to make me well), and I lay back waiting. I didn't question anyone, working as I always used to on the philosophy that "You're the doctor, make me better, tell me how much I owe you and I'll see you around the pool." To tell you the truth, I wasn't frightened either. Friends have often said that they would have been terrified in the same situation, but I wasn't. The fact is I love hospitals, I really do. When that hospital room door is shut, I feel safe, confident that everyone in the building is taking care of me, from the lady in the flower shop in the lobby all the way up to the big-shot doctors.

After two days I was almost beginning to enjoy myself. The routine that other people find boring I found almost exciting. Relaxation is a luxury I have rarely indulged in, so to be compelled to wallow in it came as a gift from heaven. Even checking off the items on the little menu card that came around at mealtimes was a pleasure, and the food was very good.

I think that after all the glamour of restaurants with rich delicacies, a good plain simple meal can be very exciting. . . .

Then into this comfortable scene walked the villain. In my doorway appeared four people, led by Dr. Kenneth

Black—a specialist, as I later discovered, in diabetes. I suddenly felt a twinge of alarm, bordering on outright fear, as with a great deal of studied carelessness Dr. Black said, "Well, we've come to the conclusion that you've got diabetes. You're not, I'm afraid, going to be able to get rid of it, so you'll have to learn to live with it." Half-remembering talk of "sugar diabetes" when I was a kid, I nodded and asked, "What is diabetes?" A fair question, I thought. . . .

So they told me.

2

Comes the Dawn...
Sort Of

My doctors talked and I listened, and gradually a picture of the disease that was to change me in so many ways began to emerge. I did not learn everything straight away. In fact, I reckon that I learn more and more about diabetes with every day that passes. But to begin with, I imbibed a few basic facts.

Diabetes, they told me, is a shortened form of *diabetes mellitus*, meaning literally "honeyed urine" (from the Latin). Whereas sugar coming from foods is, in the normal individual, broken down and used as an energy supply, the diabetic's system is such that there is a buildup of sugar. Excessive amounts accumulating in the blood then have deleterious effects on the body in general. You see, even my vocabulary is improving.

Well, forgetting the effects for the moment, my first reaction was to ask, "What causes this sugar saturation?" In other words, "What's wrong with me?" A simple question, you might think, but one that prompted a careful and enlightening answer, involving a mini-lesson on the way that often abused food processing plant we call the body works when supplied with the proper nourishment.

Sugar, in the form of glucose, is obtained from all so-called starchy foods—carbohydrates—that regularly make

7

up part of our diet: bread, potatoes, rice, pasta, cakes, puddings, jams and preserves, candy, cookies, and fruit. When eaten, the carbohydrates are digested in the stomach and intestines and converted into glucose. This is then absorbed into the bloodstream, so that the blood sugar level rises. It would continue to rise, spilling over into the urine, were it not taken up and used as energy by the cells of the body to build new tissue. The glucose that is not needed immediately is stored in the liver, to be drawn upon when required. Gradually excess sugar not used up is laid down as fat (or *adipose tissue*).

What goes wrong with the diabetic is this crucial energy conversion process, so that the blood sugar continues to stick around. And the reason for the breakdown in the mechanism is a fault in the body's capacity to produce correctly a vital substance: insulin. It is insulin that enables glucose to become available as an energy source for the many millions of cells in the body, in ways, incidentally, that are still not fully understood. The diabetic either does not produce enough insulin or has "resistance" to the action of that insulin at the cellular level to use foods properly.

That, in short, was diabetes. But why me? Then again, why not me? Anyway, I put that question to the doctor a few days later, days in which I lay mulling over the situation, trying to feel like Bette Davis in *Dark Victory* but, just between you and me, sorry for myself. Anyway, I began to learn a few more basic facts and experienced a mixture of curiosity and surprise when I found out that the type of diabetes I had managed to acquire was usually found only in children. But more of that in a moment. For the present there am I, propped up in bed in the London Clinic, being regularly injected with that all-too-vital insulin, when who should stroll through the doorway but one of London's most extravagant, witty, and original fellows,

Quentin Crisp. I had seen *The Naked Civil Servant* on television and fallen in love with Quentin because, leaving aside all the folderols and all the scurrilously controversial subject matter that he was talking about, the man had a quality that attracted me: a sense of blatant honesty. He seemed to be a simple person in the best sense of the word and a most exciting human being.

I had mentioned to a friend, Nadia Chigerovitch, when I was first admitted to the hospital something about thinking about Quentin Crisp because there was nothing phony about him and when you get sick and a bit frightened you think about people who are real and make sense to you. She said, "Well, that's very interesting because he's a friend of mine and he said to me yesterday that he had read in the paper that you had diabetes and were at the London Clinic and he would so love to come and visit you."

Isn't life extraordinary and sometimes terrific? Well, it was arranged and all the nurses were falling down and picking themselves up again and putting lipstick on, which I thought was terribly funny, and I warned them that Quentin probably wouldn't notice it but might want to borrow it. (The lipstick, that is.) Anyway, they were all very excited about the idea of his coming, and he didn't let them down. He came in with his slouch John Barrymore hat and pink tie and gray shirt and umbrella. I'd never met him before in my life and I'd never seen a live performance, only read about him and seen him on television. He sat down and talked to me and lifted my spirits in a way I cannot describe to you, but I will: he just seemed genuinely interested.

"Why do you think you have this disease, diabetes?" he said. "Well, let's not call it a disease, Elaine. You're just slowing down for a bit, but you'll pick up again." He said many things that were pertinent to me because diabetes *is* "slowing down for a bit," getting a new idea of what kind of gas to use for your future trips in the car and learning how to take the gas, learning how to do it and getting on with it. He instilled no fear in me at all. He was just a pleasant, wonderful, interesting guy to talk to. Anyway, to begin with, I was a little bit nervous with Quentin, because when you meet someone who's totally real (and there are an awful lot of people who aren't) you have to get real with them, although you're so used to putting on an act. There was no act necessary with him, so I soon felt very comfortable. He had a star quality about him.

I did want to get the subject off me because there I was sitting up in a hospital bed and looking a bit Queen of the May and the one that all the attention was being focused on. I don't know why I chose this question, but we talked for almost an hour, and in the course of the conversation I asked him, "Quentin, when you were a little boy, what did you want to be when you grew up?"

"An invalid," he said, and I almost fell out of the hospital bed laughing. As soon as I recovered I got the idea that this man had had very little love in his early years and he must have felt that if he became an invalid he'd get love and attention. What better way . . . oh, Quentin, what sadder way? But what an honest guy to admit that about himself.

If I never meet him again I will treasure that hour with him. Incidentally, we were served tea, compliments of the London Clinic, and I noticed the cakes were a little different. They were fancier and more scrumptious than the ones served for all my other guests during my stay in the hospital.

Quite a charmer, old Quentin. If you don't believe me, ask the nurses.

3
Hanging In There

I understood in general terms about my body's recently acquired inability to handle sugar properly, and how this was linked to some kind of malfunctioning in the insulin department. Beyond that, though, there was a fog of ignorance that I wanted desperately to dispel. A glimmer of enlightenment began to dawn when I learned that diabetics fall into two main groups. The first are those suffering from the so-called severe or juvenile type of diabetes (also known as Type I or ketotic diabetes), which, as its name implies, affects mostly youngsters. It is due to a total lack of insulin production, something triggered off by a childhood infection such as a virus, and strikes often with dramatic suddenness, with the following symptoms:

- More urine than normal is passed, sometimes noticed in youngsters through bed-wetting. This in turn compels the diabetic to drink more fluids.
- Loss of weight is commonplace, even though the young diabetic is eating normally. Regular growth is also impaired until the child is treated for the condition.
- Emotional changes are seen, such as irritable behavior in a usually happy infant.
- Drowsiness or even coma may ensue if the condition is left untreated.

The second type of diabetes, sometimes called mild or maturity-onset diabetes and also known as Type II or nonketotic diabetes, affects by far the majority of diabetics—around 85 percent—who are able to produce insulin but not enough of it to break down the sugar.

One of the striking facts about mild diabetes is its relationship to obesity. When adults succumb to the disease they are often overweight. Obesity by itself leads to a relative resistance to the action of insulin at the level of the cell. When obesity is coupled with a hereditary predisposition, overt diabetes may result. Also, as we get older, our sensitivity to insulin declines. The symptoms are similar, but may be more insidious:

- Tiredness and a general feeling of physical and mental sluggishness.
- The need to urinate at night, again coupled with a powerful thirst that makes you need to drink every quarter of an hour or so.
- Weight loss.

Now, statistically speaking, you would think that my chances of falling into this second category were pretty high; I was after all not a child or teenager. Neither had I been struck down by some debilitating virus infection that might have wrought havoc with my hitherto robust insulin-producing plant. However, despite the odds, my diabetes, said Dr. Black, was of the juvenile type, which, as well as being the more serious, meant that I would have to rely on insulin injections permanently. Not for me a quick weight loss program with fresh air, exercise, and a planned diet. Elaine Stritch was now cast in the role of "diabetic," and I decided that this particular "play" was going to have a long run, the rest of my life.

The causes of diabetes of both the severe and mild

types are, it appears, the subject of some discussion among doctors and researchers, but as yet no one can say with any certainty where every case of diabetes originated. Insulin, a hormone, or chemical messenger, is made in the pancreas in special tiny factories called *beta cells*. So if, for some reason, a person had to have the entire pancreas removed, there would be no insulin production, and diabetes would ensue. On rare occasions, a definite link between an antecedent viral infection and diabetes can be made. However, in most cases the cause is speculative. In some countries of the world there is a virus that attacks the pancreas specifically, so again insulin production is impaired. Excessive alcohol consumption can sometimes have the same effect, if it is carried on for many years. In all those cases it is not difficult for doctors to find the cause of diabetes. But in most cases it is not that easy. Those beta cells can be rendered ineffective by a cause or causes unknown.

There are clearly hereditary factors operating that predispose some individuals to succumb to the disease. It has been estimated that 25 percent of the American population either have diabetes, will have it, or have had a diabetic relative. Nonetheless, the fact that hereditary factors play a part does not mean that one is necessarily born a diabetic if, say, both parents have the disease. If both parents have Type II (maturity-onset) diabetes, there is a one-in-three chance of their child developing diabetes, and then usually during middle age. If only one parent has the disease, the chances are considerably less. In my case, neither of my parents was diabetic, so I cannot directly blame the genes I received from them for my condition. Nevertheless, there must have been a *tendency*, if no more than that, toward diabetes in my bodily makeup from birth, a tendency that was brought out into the open by something later in life.

The most compelling evidence for a hereditary factor

comes from the studies of diabetes in identical twins. If one twin develops maturity-onset, non-insulin-dependent diabetes, the other twin will also ultimately develop diabetes nearly 100 percent of the time. However, the statistics for juvenile-onset (insulin-dependent) diabetes are not as striking. There the concordance rate is somewhere between 20 and 50 percent.

Another possibility is that there is a viral component to juvenile diabetes, with a virus acting as a trigger in susceptible individuals. There is a seasonal variation in the onset of diabetes that corresponds to peak epidemics of certain viruses. The association with preceding bouts of mumps, hepatitis, and infectious mononucleosis is more than coincidental. Further support for a viral hypothesis comes from animal models, particularly certain strains of mice.

Another contributory element in my own path into diabetes—and this really is a personal point of view—is that I believe I have what I would call a "diabetic personality." I think extremists tend to get the disease more than middle-of-the-roaders, those easy-going types who never seem to be in the thrall of emotional ups and downs. It occurs to me in retrospect that whenever I got ill or sick it was as a result of an emotional state of mind or of something that happened to me. After each cold, after each attack of the flu, I can look back and say, "That's why I got it." My attitude toward life, the way I'm getting along with people, the way I get through a day seem to monitor my health, and I don't think that's unique.

Some people are more prone to infection than others, and, more than with most people, my physical well-being seems to respond to my state of mind. I have had throat trouble before the opening night of every musical I've been in. Well, even a not very aware person could work out that your weakest spot is what you're most worried about. I'm very healthy. I had scarlet fever and measles as a kid. The most serious illness I ever had in my life was infectious mononucleosis—glandular fever—which is thought to be a virus infection of the central nervous system. The symptoms are very much like those of polio and they scared the hell out of everybody, certainly out of me, until they were diagnosed as mononucleosis. Perhaps this illness did play a role in my susceptibility to diabetes, as some evidence has suggested.

Right now, though, there was nothing to do but lie back and think about the events of the past few weeks: about Dr. Black and his team; about beta cells and blood sugar; about those insulin shots they were giving me twice a day. What was it they'd said about the insulin? Something about restoring the proper balance in a way that I could no longer do naturally. A proper balance. For the rest of my life. Not a bad idea, I said to myself. Okay, I'll give it a shot—or maybe even two—a day. We'll see.

4

Insulin, Here I Come

Like it or not, I had a newfound friend in the form of a remarkable substance: insulin. Twice a day, with the sort of unfailing regularity only hospitals can impose on you, a nurse would come along with her little kit of syringe, insulin, medi-swab (medicated swab), all neat in a shining kidney-shaped dish, and deliver the goods that would ensure the critical balance of blood sugar level. Not unnaturally, I began to take an interest in this substance, a drug in that it keeps people well and yet as natural as any other of the many hormones circulating in the body. In fact, so interested did I become that I took to a little background reading on the subject of insulin, especially its "discovery," if you can call it that, more than half a century ago. And a wonderful story it is, too.

Horrifying as it now seems, when in the 1920s Dr. Frederick Grant Banting of the University of Toronto in Canada began serious work on what causes diabetes, there was no treatment at all for the disease. It had been thought, however, that too much food might be implicated, since, during times of famine, near-starving populations did not seem to have diabetes. What is more, experiments dating back to the end of the nineteenth century had led some scientists to believe that diabetes was the outcome of a malfunctioning in the pancreas, the gland near the stomach responsible for producing digestive juices to help break

17

down food. In fact, a certain Dr. Langerhans, a German medical researcher, had discovered that some cells in the pancreas in what he called "islets" of tissue seemed to differ from the rest. And it was later discovered, this time in the United States, that these *islets of Langerhans* had deteriorated in some diabetes sufferers.

So far so good, but why should the condition of these islets have anything to do with raised blood sugar? A British doctor provided the answer in 1916 when he speculated that perhaps these islets were not producing a necessary digestive juice, which he called, appropriately, *insuline*, after the Latin word *insula*, meaning "an island." The explanation was fine. But the problems came in isolating some "insuline" to test it out.

Enter next the single-minded Dr. Banting, who started to do some experiments, in a borrowed laboratory incidentally, aided by a young student called Charles Best. The year was 1921. By the summer they had managed to extract some material from the pancreas of animals that seemed to be of use in restoring the health of a diabetic dog, Mayone. Yes, dogs, too, can be afflicted with diabetes and are still of use in helping researchers. At Guy's Hospital in London, for example, the scientists enlisted the services of a poodle, Roger, who became, according to Peter Mason of the *Daily Express*, a VIP (Very Important Pooch). The following is from the *Daily Express*, Monday, February 2 (my birthday), 1981:

ROGER THE VERY IMPORTANT POOCH DOES HIS BIT FOR MEDICAL RESEARCH

Roger the Poodle is a cut above his canine contemporaries. While other dogs go walkies, he travels by Rolls-Royce and eats only the best lamb and fish. But then Roger is a VIP—a Very Important Pooch. He is diabetic.

After ten years of daily insulin injections Roger was not suffering from any of the side effects that afflict human diabetics. Roger led a normal active life and did not suffer cataracts on the eyes—a common complaint among human diabetics.

He was such a medical rarity that doctors at Guy's Hospital, London, gave him a special pass, making him the only dog allowed in. The doctors who are doing research into retinopathy—diseases of the retina—were using Roger in their probe into the causes of cataracts. The research is being carried out by a team under Professor Harry Keen, who said that Roger's cooperation "was of great benefit to the human race." Once a month Roger left the home he shared in Pagham, West Sussex, with his owner, wealthy widow Mrs. Katherine Cosmo Cran, for a chauffeur-driven ride to London by Rolls-Royce.

LAVISHED

Mrs Cosmo Cran said of chauffeur Arthur Wigmore: "He's been with me twenty years, and he was really marvellous with Roger."

She added: "I'd given Roger his insulin injection every day since he contracted diabetes nine years ago, when he was just a puppy.

"No dog had lived to Roger's age with diabetes before and the doctors all say that it is due to the care and attention I lavished on him during the time he was ill."

Professor Keen hopes that the close monitoring of Roger's progress will help to discover why human diabetics develop cataracts.

Anyway, more of eye disorders and diabetes later. For the moment, let's go back to Banting and Best. So, they had extracted a substance that would help dogs. What next? The following January, 1922, an eleven-year-old acutely diabetic boy named Leonard Thompson made history when he was injected with the new material and showed signs of a dramatic improvement. His diabetes was controlled. Had the newly named insulin not come to his aid, Leonard might have been faced with the frightening prospect of a stringent diet, coma, and eventually a long-drawn-out death. Instead he could expect normality, and so could millions of others after him. And that, thank you very much, includes me!

Actually, the insulin story does not end there. It really only just begins, and I shall be saying a bit more about research into more effective ways of producing and using it later on. For the moment, though, I'd like to dwell on the two men who have, literally, saved more lives than anyone has been able to count, Banting and Best. And I'd like to explain how I see insulin having its effects.

Imagine that the food you eat to provide energy is like the electricity running to your house or apartment. The mains are all there. To use the energy available, all that's needed is a flick of the switch. In the body, insulin is what does the switching on. The flow of insulin from the pancreas speeds up the use of sugar by the body, in the same way that the electricity meter turns more quickly when you have all the domestic lights and appliances running. Insulin also helps to store this sugar (in the form of fat) and to manufacture proteins that are necessary for all living organisms, in building muscle, for example. After each meal, the level of sugar in the blood rises bit by bit until the natural flow of insulin ensures that it is maintained at a controlled level. In the nondiabetic, this means a blood sugar level somewhere in the region of 110 milligrams per 100 milliliters of blood, never rising above about 150 mg per 100 ml even after a big meal. The rate of insulin secretion is regulated by the demands put on the digestive system, so that, for example, just after breakfast the nondiabetic will have an insulin "high" to cope with the sudden influx of glucose in the bloodstream after the fasting period during the night. It's as if a sudden thunderstorm on a bright, sunny day had forced you to switch on all the lights in the house.

With the diabetic there are not enough insulin switches or, if there are, they do not work properly. After breakfast the blood sugar level shoots up, but there is no corresponding upturn in insulin production. A mild diabetic—that is, someone who is on the borderline—may have a blood sugar level nearing 200 mg per 100 ml after breakfast, while the true out-and-out full-fledged diabetic escalates to 300 mg per 100 ml and beyond.

It has been estimated that for every two people known to be in this latter category, there is at least one other on the borderline, which means to all intents and purposes an "unrecognized diabetic."

One way in which doctors can pick out these borderline cases is by measuring what they call the *fasting blood sugar level*—that is, directly after a person has got up in the morning but *before* breakfast. All of us vary from day to day, because the human metabolism does not run with the clockwork predictability of a machine, but if the fasting plasma glucose is greater than 140 mg per 100 ml on two separate occasions, then diabetes may be present. If, in addition, the plasma sugar is greater than 200 mg per 100 ml on two occasions after a 75 gram oral glucose challenge (a controlled test), then diabetes can definitely be diagnosed (these guidelines follow the latest criteria of the National Diabetes Data Group of the National Institutes of Health).

Below 100 mg per 100 ml, and again there's usually no doubt. The person is not diabetic. The problem with labeling someone as having borderline, or "chemical" diabetes is that many of these people will never progress to the full-fledged disease. Many factors, including illness, anxiety, and inadequate diet in preparation for the glucose tolerance test, may render it falsely positive, alarming someone needlessly.

In my case, though, there was no doubt; so I simply had to counteract the excess sugar by taking insulin. In the early days in the hospital, as I said earlier, the injections presented no problem. Then came the bombshell.

It was getting on to the last week in the hospital and they had me pretty well balanced. I had three or four nurses, one of whom I liked particularly. Her name was Kim Ong. She was Chinese, need I say, and she was adorable. One of those sunshine people, a breath of fresh air—I loved her. She was assigned to give me my morning injection. One morning she said, "You go home sunny [Sunday]. I think now you start injecting in you, yourself . . . now!"

I almost fainted with fear at the thought of sticking that needle in . . . all by myself and I . . . alone. She was so straightforward about it all and so sweet and adorable that I said, "Okay, what the hell . . . Kim, you're on!" But it's amazing now to think how scared I was. It just shows what we can learn to do in life if we have to.

I hadn't really been paying much attention to the injections, probably subconsciously trying to shy away from them. She came over to my bed and sat down beside me. She said, "Now, take needo with sa-ringe outo pak. No touch nowhere! Take medi-swab, clean good, cap on botto. Then stick in needo, push aio [air] swo. Poo down easy and snap fingoes to lif aio bubbos. No . . . aio bubbos! Velly danjo'us to have aio bubbos. Now pinch up little skin and like you sew with needo. Velly easy . . . stick into leg . . . needo . . . you do . . . easy . . . do. Now!"

I was crying and laughing at the same time and she was saying, "Easy, velly easy . . . you do easy." So I took the needle and I did it very slowly, like a beginner at a Singer sewing machine class, and I put it in. . . . Hooray! I didn't hurt myself and I put my little finger up the plunger and went *zap*. In it went. I took the needle out very gently, put the medi-swab over it, and jumped out of the bed—I did it, I did it! I was jumping around the room like a six-year-old kid.

I really felt at that point there was nothing in this world I couldn't tackle. I jumped back in bed and said, "Oh, Kim, I'm so proud and happy I did it . . . I did it!" Meanwhile she was gathering up the debris, swab and needle, etc., and she'd got it all on the little tray. As she walked to the door, she turned back to me and said, "I wouldn't do that to myself for anything in the world!" Getting diabetes was almost worth that line.

For the rest of the week I didn't look forward to injecting myself, but I did do it and I knew it was the right thing to do. I had to get used to doing it before I left the hospital, for, believe me, there would be no Kim Ong at the Savoy! Waiters in room service maybe, but I don't think insulin injections are part of their training.

Toward the end of that week I was getting such confidence from the fact that I was doing it that I would ask the nurse to stay outside so that I'd feel totally alone with the needle; then I'd do it and have her come back in again afterward, so I didn't have "mother" there to hang on to. That was pretty clever of me because it got me used to injecting myself totally on my own. The next really frightening moment was indeed sitting on the side of my bed at home and doing it alone. When I was in the hospital the doctor had talked constantly to my husband, John, to fill him in on a few things he could expect to find, in me, and about me, with diabetes. I was half-asleep one day in the hospital, and my husband was sitting in the corner on a chair with an orange and a lemon, which I had practiced on, and I saw John saying, "Oh, there's nothing to this, you just have to . . ." and he's jamming this needle into the orange like it *was* an orange and not my bum, and he said, "I've got this down to a system now, there's nothing to it."

I looked over and I thought to myself: John is not going to inject me unless we're on a desert island and both of my arms are broken. Then, and only then, could he have a shot at it, if you'll pardon the pun!

5

The Balancing Act of All Time

Being a diabetic means taking responsibility for your own medical destiny. It is the do-it-yourself illness *par excellence*. There was a long-running British TV documentary series about surgery called "Your Life in Their Hands." Well, with diabetes it is your life in *your* hands. You become—even if like me you have no intention, inclination, or apparent ability to do so—your own physician.

There is an old saying among the doctors: "Know syphilis, know medicine," which is an abbreviated way of conveying the idea that by understanding the causes, effects, diagnosis, and treatment of this particular disease, one understands much about the whole of the doctor's art and craft. It is a neat way of putting it, except that currently many doctors are inclined to think that a better source of insight might be diabetes. Few other diseases are linked with such a wide variety of bodily processes; few give such a broad view of how our metabolism works and what the repercussions are of its going wrong. In those earth-moving few weeks between learning that I had diabetes and being discharged from the London Clinic to set about trying to lead a normal life again, I had reached several important conclusions.

The first was that I was absolutely determined that nothing, but nothing, was going to prevent me from continuing to do what I had always wanted to do: be an actress. Not diabetes, not anything.

Second, if I was to realize that ambition I would have to do so in a spirit not of bravado but of common sense. I was not going to rush at the enemy to take him by storm, but triumph with subtlety and skill, born of knowledge. That meant sitting back awhile and learning as much as I could about the condition: when it was particularly dangerous; how I could cope with it at times of stress or work pressure; where it was taking me in the long term.

Third—and this was perhaps the single most telling conclusion I reached—I was going to adopt the old Boy Scout motto and "Be Prepared." Life from now on, I figured, was simply too serious, too precious, and too risky to be left to chance. Operation Organization was launched in a big way. Looking back, I can see that I probably felt the way most people feel when told they have a serious, incurable illness—a combination of alarm and determination. There was nothing special in my feelings. Where I did feel disadvantaged, though, was in the thought that my profession seemed not to have been designed for the diabetes sufferer. It is hectic, unpredictable, full of worries both major and petty, and above all not characterized by routine existence.

Apart from being shown how to give myself insulin, I had also been given a guide to diet and exercise (about which more later), which on the face of it looked pretty hard to reconcile with an intensive few day's rehearsals or taping or whatever. But again, with hindsight, I can see that my fears were exaggerated. It was and still is possible to do a job with irregular hours, under trying circumstances, in unfamiliar surroundings, as a diabetic. I know because I'm doing it.

So step one—which you must take—is to be clear in your own mind that you *can* cope with your diabetes. Only the "How?" remains to be worked out in detail.

Step two is to try to understand a little more about the disease, with the help of what follows. This is not a textbook, as you will have noticed, so don't expect to find every minute question answered. After all, there are something like 20–30 million diabetics worldwide, each an individual with particular responses to the disease. That makes an awful lot of experts with something to contribute over and above anything I might say.

One thing has to be said, though. There is more, a lot more, to having diabetes than being careful about keeping those blood sugar levels down to a safe amount. The U.S. National Commission on Diabetes carried out a survey on the possible long-term effects, "late complications," as they called them, of the disease and found that a diabetic has:

25 times greater risk than the nondiabetic of blindness;

17 times the risk of kidney failure;

17 times the risk of gangrene.

These long-term complications seem to be the end product of years of rapid fluctuations in blood glucose levels, and these can develop if the diabetes is unchecked by any form of sugar control, whether by diet, pills, or injections.

Changes in vision are very commonplace, though often scarcely noticed in those early days before diabetes has been diagnosed. Many people—and I'm lucky here in that I have not had this experience—find that their vision is blurred or dimmed. They are watching television, say, and when they look away to pick up a cup, the scene suddenly fuzzes over. Or they find that they are getting even more nearsighted than they used to be and may be forced to visit the optician for a new pair of glasses that help them to focus better on distant objects. Even people who have not been wearing glasses may over a period find that their distance vision is impaired, though they are probably more concerned about the fact that they are excessively thirsty or losing weight to worry specifically about visual defects that lots of other perfectly healthy people also have.

What appears to cause these disturbances is a number of changes in the lens of the eye as a result of the accumulation of sugars. The lens literally swells up, thereby making it more difficult for the near-to-distant focusing mechanism to function as it should. There is, however, no need to worry unduly about all this because, within a few weeks of getting onto a regime of proper blood glucose balance, the blurring and so on should gradually disappear. And then you may need to hunt through your drawers to find those old glasses you recently discarded!

There are some diabetics whose visual problems take a slightly different form. They may have had no blurred vision before treatment, but begin to notice deterioration, surprisingly enough, *after* it begins. And this happens sometimes very rapidly, even overnight. Again, though, these changes, brought about by temporary modifications in the lens and retina, will usually subside in 4 to 6 weeks.

More serious are those long-term effects I mentioned a moment ago. Occasionally they affect people who have been suffering for ten years or more and—this is the important part—have not had consistently good control over the condition. Unlike those transitory effects, these are not so easy to reverse. Seven out of ten very long-standing diabetics have suffered damage to the lens in the form of cataracts or to the eyeball in the form of glaucoma (high pressure). Five percent of diabetics develop glaucoma, as compared with 2 percent of people in the nondiabetic population. A person with diabetes is five times more likely to develop cataracts at a younger age than the normal population. Vision is inevitably going to deteriorate if these occur.

Most serious of all, though (even if it only affects a minority), is damage to the blood vessels of the retina at the back of the eye, which sometimes leads to blindness. This retinopathy, as it is called, can even detach the retina from its base. Almost all diabetics will have some degree of retinopathy after twenty years of diabetes. Retinopathy can be classified as proliferative or nonproliferative. *Nonproliferative retinopathy* includes tiny hemorrhages and areas of poor blood flow. *Proliferative retinopathy* is the most serious, consisting of new blood vessels on the surface of the retina. These vessels are very fragile and prone to hemorrhage.

The reason I have cataloged some of the eye problems of the diabetic is to tell not a horror story but a cautionary tale. The better you manage to control the condition, the less chance there is of major visual handicaps hitting you. The earlier you spot and report to your doctor any signs of trouble (and that means regular eye checkups in just the same way as you have periodic dental checkups), the more successful will be the treatment. And if the worst does seem to be happening, advanced surgical techniques for refixing detached retinas or laser-sealing leaking blood vessels may be used to forestall it. Although diabetic eye disease is the leading cause of new blindness in the United States, the very effective treatment now available for many of the complications caused by diabetes shows that the outlook for diabetics' vision is not quite as bleak as it appears.

The same is true of kidney problems. Once again, changes in the small blood vessels within the kidneys are to blame for the urinary conditions. High blood sugar over a long period of time damages some of the million filtration units, called *glomeruli*, in each kidney that are responsible for ridding the blood of waste products to be disposed of in the urine. If these glomeruli break down, waste material, *urea*, builds up, poisoning the blood and making you feel excessively tired. Alternatively you may suffer retention of urine, and edema, with swelling around the ankles.

Once more, unless blood sugar level control has been poor for too long, the outlook is promising. Although probably more than a quarter of all long-term diabetics—that is, people who have been diabetic for twenty-five years or more—experience some kidney complaints, these are usually not serious enough to make them feel positively unwell. Prompt treatment coupled with proper diabetic control, as well as vigilant attention to any signs of urinary infection suggested by symptoms such as cystitis, prevent irreversible kidney damage and the more lasting forms of discomfort.

Moving down the anatomy, from eyes to kidneys to feet, we come to yet another potential danger area for the diabetic. For doctors, diabetes and foot problems are almost synonymous. Diabetics are more prone to foot problems because of either infection, changes in the nerves, or poor circulation. So proper foot care is critical, with attention to purchasing properly fitting shoes, learning how to trim toenails correctly, forgoing walking barefoot, and daily foot inspection. As we get older, all of us, diabetic or not, may notice that poor blood circulation produces pain in the calf and foot muscles when walking or when standing. With diabetics, this tendency may be aggravated by painful sensations in the feet such as acute tingling, or by the opposite experience, namely, numbness to pain so that you do not even notice a minor injury or infection. What has happened here is that the buildup of excess sugar in the bloodstream has affected the nerves in the legs and feet, as well as blocking the production of a special substance needed by nerves to function properly. This means that these nerves are simply unable to carry all the right messages to the brain or to the muscles, so that instead of, say, feeling pain, you are insensitive to a stimulus. Once again, blood sugar control can dispel pins and needles and other forms of sensitivity in the legs and feet, but if the damage has been left unchecked for too long, perhaps for twenty years or more, it may be irreversible. As well as feeling strange sensations, the long-term diabetic may find that the muscles become weak and a condition known as *foot drop* sets in, whereby you cannot even lift your feet.

Actually, the tendency for diabetes to affect nerves can also be seen elsewhere in the body. After all, many functions of the body that we take for granted as "automatic" are of course under the control of the autonomic nervous system—emptying the bladder or stomach, for example. Diabetically caused nervous damage can show itself in a whole host of symptoms from diarrhea to the inability in men to obtain an erection.

All in all, then, diabetics can be prone to a range of later complications, but that in itself is not cause for despondency. It has certainly not made *me* go into a faint-hearted decline at the thought of possible future dangers, because I know that it lies in my hands to reduce my chances of succumbing to them. Remember these encouraging words from a publication of the British Diabetic Association:

> . . . Only a very small proportion of diabetics suffer from the complications, and these can usually be prevented by good control at all times. This is especially important in the young diabetic with many years of life ahead. Prevention of these complications is always better and easier than treatment when they occur.

I will be talking a bit more about prevention later on, but for now I want just to stress the importance of correct blood sugar balance: in the immediate present, to enable you to live a normal life, whether "normal" for you means the calm, regular routines of a librarian or the strenuous, even chaotic, ups and downs of the actress; in the long term, to prevent the onset of those complications, some of which are too obviously serious to need further elaboration from me.

I've been blithely saying that diabetics need "good control" over their condition as if it were always self-evident what this control really means. But many newly diagnosed diabetics have trouble with the phrase because they mistakenly feel that the sole aim is to lower blood sugar levels. Instead, they should be aiming for balance. If the distinction seems no more than a play upon words, perhaps I should explain what control and balance are all about and, more the practical point, how you can be sure you are achieving them.

In a healthy body, the insulin production system is perfectly geared to the demands of the moment. Just after a meal the level of insulin rises dramatically to cope with this sudden input of sugar, but falls rapidly when it is no longer needed. In other words, there is what the politicians would call a beautifully balanced supply-and-demand situation, far better tuned than any economy in the world. Peaks and troughs in blood sugar levels are matched, shoulder to shoulder, by the corresponding hormone—insulin—that regulates them.

We have established that the diabetic is insulin-deficient in some way. Let's see how this condition, if uncontrolled, might upset this "delicate balance," to use Edward Albee's phrase. One effect might be that you begin to develop *hyperglycemia*, which is just another way of saying "high blood sugar." You may begin to feel ill, perhaps because you are overeating or have had some sort of infection, or even because you're emotionally upset. Or you may simply have forgotten to take your pills or injections. Conversely, you may develop the opposite condition, *hypoglycemia*, "low blood sugar," because the amount of insulin you have been taking is not being matched by a balancing input of food. You may have forgotten to eat or have been too rushed to eat at the right time. Or you may have burned up too much sugar through strenuous exercise without remembering to put it back with food. Sometimes a mild diabetic who is not taking insulin can experience a hypoglycemic episode—or hypo—because his or her pancreas is too slow to produce insulin. It reaches a peak only after it is needed, that is, after the blood sugar level has already fallen, perhaps in the wake of a post-meal high.

Although only transitory, these hypos are extremely distressing. I remember having had a very hardworking, stressful day in New York, then going to a party in the evening to see a lot of old friends. I hadn't seen many of them for five or ten years, because I'd been living in Britain, so I guess I got pretty emotional. When I got home to my hotel I took my usual snack of twenty grams of carbohydrates—two shredded wheat and half a cup of milk and some Sweet 'n Low on it. All seemed fine and I went to sleep. In the middle of the night I had a hypo. Now, I've had hypos in my sleep a couple of times since and have always woken up and known what to do. But this one went too far. I had the shock of my life. I woke up, and all I could remember was that I wanted to go to the bathroom. As I got out of bed I fell down, hitting the floor so hard my husband woke up. I was really out of commission. I couldn't move, my hands were turning in, and my feet were turning in as if I had polio. I was fully conscious. John lifted me onto the bed, and though I tried to talk to him I lost all sense of speech. I was literally dumbstruck. And the interesting thing was, it never occurred to me it was because I was diabetic. John did make the connection and said, "You've got to eat something." As for me, I thought I had had a stroke, and that "something else" had hit me. I simply didn't attribute those peculiar symptoms to diabetes. John meanwhile was trying to get me to eat some sugar, which I refused because of my highly disciplined attitude toward diabetes. "It's not time for me to have my carbohydrates," I managed to say. "I haven't had my injection yet." John then really got mad and said, "You eat this or I'll kill you." So I did, and in twenty minutes I was fine.

The symptoms I have experienced with hypos, on the mercifully few occasions I have had them, include numbness and tingling in the limbs, loss of speech, sweating and nausea, nervousness, pounding in the heart, loss of memory and mental confusion, and headaches. And unlike hypers, these hypoglycemic attacks strike rapidly.

An even more serious effect of poor diabetic control is a coma, something that so far (and I'm knocking on wood for all I'm worth now) I have not experienced. What causes some comas is a condition known as *ketoacidosis*, in which the body is unable to use up or store energy in the form of fats. The excess of fats spills over as fragments of material called *ketones*. These build up to ever-higher levels, producing symptoms of rapid breathing and nausea, followed by thirst, an unusually frequent desire to pass water, listlessness, and finally sleepiness followed sometimes by loss of consciousness. Left unchecked, this accumulation of ketones in the blood can, after just a few days or even hours, be so serious as to be life-threatening. Ketoacidosis-type comas are usually confined to children. But adults, too, can suffer comas through prolonged hyperglycemia. The warning signs are, again, thirst, fatigue, urination frequency increase, and changes in one's breathing rates, all due to the persistently elevated levels of sugar and ketones in the blood and urine. And by elevated levels I mean really elevated: up to twenty or thirty times that of a normal person.

So much, then, for this idea of diabetic control and the sometimes harrowing effects of relinquishing it. A recently developed test—the *hemoglobin A1C level* or *glycohemoglobin level*—can help you and your doctor determine the adequacy of your control over the preceding weeks. What happens is that sugar in the blood reacts slowly with the hemoglobin protein in the red blood cells to produce an irreversible change. By measuring what percentage of the hemoglobin has been modified, you can gauge how good control was for the four to eight weeks before the specimen was drawn. Normal individuals have a 5–7 percent hemoglobin A1C (actually properly A_{1C}) level, whereas the less-controlled diabetic may have a value ranging from 12 percent to 16 percent.

On an everyday basis I and all diabetics have to know what the state of our bodily balance actually is at any time. You soon begin to know when you have lost control, but how do you ascertain the degree of control you are retaining? From what I've been saying it should be clear that all these extreme episodes of comas and the like can be prevented by managing your diabetes. And the better the management, the more remote are the chances of even minor discomforts troubling you. So here is my patent do-it-yourself kit for monitoring my own bodily condition. In later chapters I'll be telling you how I endeavor to maintain it.

ITEM ONE   is a telephone. I call my doctor and arrange for regular medical checkups. This is something every diabetic has to do with unfailing certainty, however adept you may feel you have become at keeping your own medical house in order. In fact I can't stress the importance of this too strongly, for several reasons. First, the very fact that you meet regularly with your doctor puts a little more onus on you to try to maintain good control. Second, your diabetes may, over a period of years, produce the need for slightly different treatments, which only your doctor can detect and prescribe. And third, there is the point I discussed earlier about the long-term effects on health of diabetes that is not properly controlled. If there has been any damage, you and your doctor need to know as soon as possible so that it does not prove to be irreversible. Here's how one expert sums up the relationship you should be developing:

> Control of diabetes depends on intelligent co-operation between patient and doctor. There must be a two-way exchange of ideas between the diabetic and doctor as each can learn from the other. *The diabetic should understand his own diabetes, and the doctor can help him to learn.*

Now back to my control kit.

ITEM TWO is a reliable set of bathroom scales. It is worth investing in good, strong scales. They last longer and give a reading that you can use with confidence to help control your diabetes. The fact is—and I'll be talking more about this later—there is a strong association between obesity and diabetes. In my case this has never been the problem in that I am one of nature's slimliners, but nevertheless, it is necessary even for people built like me to watch their weight, for I can gain weight at the drop of a Mars Bar. By getting on the scales once or twice a week, preferably in roughly the same clothes and at the same time of day, I can tell whether my weight is fluctuating at all. I jot down the readings in a little pad in the bathroom, and if there is a persistent up or down trend over a week or two I talk to my doctor about it. There are lots of people who will give you advice about what constitutes the "ideal" weight for your height and build, but personally I've found it much more useful to consult the charts produced by the Metropolitan Life Insurance Company in New York (see the charts that follow). They tell you what

DESIRABLE WEIGHTS

(Weight in Pounds According to Frame, in Indoor Clothing; Shoes with 1″ Heels)

Men of Ages 25 and Over			
Height Feet Inches	Small Frame	Medium Frame	Large Frame
5 2	128–134	131–141	138–150
5 3	130–136	133–143	140–153
5 4	132–138	135–145	142–156
5 5	134–140	137–148	144–160
5 6	136–142	139–151	146–164
5 7	138–145	142–154	149–168
5 8	140–148	145–157	152–172
5 9	142–151	148–160	155–176
5 10	144–154	151–163	158–180
5 11	146–157	154–166	161–184
6 0	149–160	157–170	164–188
6 1	152–164	160–174	168–192
6 2	155–168	164–178	172–197
6 3	158–172	167–182	176–202
6 4	162–176	171–187	181–207

are sensible average weights for your height, frame, and age bracket, and for the diabetic—who should never exceed the average—are an easy-to-follow guide.

Average Weight of Adults

These tables were constructed from statistical data published in the 1979 Build Study, Society of Actuaries and Association of Life Insurance Medical Directors of America. They are reproduced by kind permission of the Metropolitan Life Insurance Company, New York.

Women of Ages 25 and Over			
Height Feet Inches	**Small Frame**	**Medium Frame**	**Large Frame**
4 10	102–111	109–121	118–131
4 11	103–113	111–123	120–134
5 0	104–115	113–126	122–137
5 1	106–118	115–129	125–140
5 2	108–121	118–132	128–143
5 3	111–124	121–135	131–147
5 4	114–127	124–138	134–151
5 5	117–130	127–141	137–155
5 6	120–133	130–144	140–159
5 7	123–136	133–147	143–163
5 8	126–139	136–150	146–167
5 9	129–142	139–153	149–170
5 10	132–145	142–156	152–173
5 11	135–148	145–159	155–176
6 0	138–151	148–162	158–179

ITEM THREE   is a urine tester for detecting sugar levels. There are, in fact, several of these on the market and I have tried them all. They each have their own particular selling points, depending on your circumstances and inclinations, and you should certainly be guided in your choice by your doctor.

If you are a mild diabetic wanting a very simple indication of sugar in the urine, the Clinistix test is one that will give you a quick but rough guide. You dip the paper strip in urine and hold it in the air for 10 seconds to see if it turns purple, which shows sugar is present. It does not tell you *how much* sugar is present. For that reason I, like most people, prefer to use the Clinitest method. It takes a little longer to carry out, but it provides me with a more accurate measure of what is going on. All you need to do is collect urine in a clean container, mix five or six drops with twice the amount of water in another container such as a test tube set aside specially for the occasion, and drop in one Clinitest tablet. After the bubbling stops, count to fifteen, gently shake the tube to mix up the contents, then compare the color of the fluid (not the sediment at the bottom) with the special Clinitest color chart. The various results you get are:

blue: no sugar
green: 0.25 percent glucose
cloudy green: 0.5 percent glucose
olive: 0.75 percent glucose
yellow/brown: 1 percent glucose
orange: 2 percent glucose

There is also the so-called two-drop test to use if you want to examine more carefully urine with more than 2 percent glucose or to measure glucose loss over a given period of, say, a day. It requires another color chart. This two-drop method, incidentally, gives greater accuracy when testing children's urine.

When I'm traveling or am pressed for time, I sometimes forsake the Clinitest technique for a new type of dipstick, rather like Clinistix, called Diastix. You simply put this into a urine sample, remove it, shake it dry, and compare the color after thirty seconds to those on a chart. Again, blue indicates no sugar, and green or brown indicates sugar present, with a variety of stages in between. The single most important point to remember with Diastix is that you must wait the full thirty seconds before checking out the color match. Time it. Tes-Tape is another method available in the United States. These test paper strips stay yellow if no sugar is present in the urine sample, but turn green or blue after about sixty seconds if sugar is present.

How often do I test urine? Every morning and every night. I don't kid around. When, for example, I have tried different forms of insulin, the doctor has asked me to keep an even more careful watch on sugar levels. If I have been ill for some reason, he also reminds me to carry out frequent testing. The time of day at which you test is also important. Your doctor will suggest a time that gives the best picture of how your insulin and dieting regimes are working. So don't do a urine test at the most convenient time for you "just to get it over and done with for the day." Try, within reasonable limits, to stick to the timetable worked out for you.

Also, be careful not to jump to conclusions about the readings you get. I might come home at 4:30 P.M. and take my Clinitest and find it orange, perhaps because I hadn't gone to the john after lunch, which is very unusual for me. You can make a mistake. Thinking your blood sugar is up, you reason it's safe for you to get in the bathtub or take a long walk, but that isn't always the case because you should take your urine test and then, if it's not blue, a half hour later take it again to see what's really cooking. This is called *double voiding*, and it makes urine testing much more reliable. Another trap is that if you're reading blue you think being blue is terrific. But I have noticed sometimes (I don't know whether it's my imagination or not) that the blue color varies. When it's royal blue, it often seems to herald trouble.

Of course, these urine tests, although they provide some indication of body sugar levels, are not altogether satisfactory if you really want to monitor the state of diabetic control. The problem is this: urine testing gives information that is slightly out of date. It tells you how blood glucose levels *were*, not how at present they *are*, so if, as we saw earlier, the secret of good control is to balance insulin and blood sugar levels, it follows that urine analysis is second best to a direct measure of the amount of glucose in the blood.

ITEM FOUR   is a plasma glucose test. Until recently only doctors with hospital laboratory facilities were able to do these direct blood tests. However, it has now become possible to do them yourself, using a blood glucose meter. So far this does not form part of my own kit, but the idea does attract me because the procedures are so simple; it takes a bit of training but not much. All you need is a single drop of blood from the fingertip, which is transferred onto a chemically treated measuring strip. There are two kinds of these strips. One simply gives you a readout of blood sugar levels by reference to a color chart. The other is slightly more complicated and uses a small electrically powered meter, which can run on batteries or mains. After putting the blood onto the strip, this strip is put into the meter and a readout obtained.

With this machine you can take a series of glucose

readings on consecutive days, one working, one resting, in order to see how your patterns vary. This enables your doctor to calculate the frequency and size of your insulin injections that much more accurately to meet the demands of your body. Conversely, the ability to measure their own blood sugar levels has allowed *patients* to reduce their own glucose fluctuations considerably, as well as to identify those periods when they are specially prone to hypogly-cemic reactions, usually at night. The meter seems to me to be of particular benefit to people like the professional footballer who uses his machine to decide exactly how much sugar he needs to eat (usually in the form of choco-late bars) just before a match to prevent a coma. Pregnant women, too, are able, with the meter, to be freed from hospitalization in the last few months before D day without jeopardizing their own or their unborn child's health. Another advantage of the meter, which is probably the strongest argument of all in its favor, is the terrific psycho-logical boost it gives you by making you feel responsible for your own destiny. A pioneer of diabetic self-management, the British consultant Dr. Robert Tattersall, considers that this kind of self-help approach gives diabetics increased self-confidence and emotional stability because they have come to terms with their condition. "They feel," he says, "in control of their own bodies and no longer at the mercy of seemingly random processes."

That, then, is the hardware you need to perform your own balancing act, with one vital element missing: your insulin injection kit or your prescribed pills. I have deliber-ately omitted them from this chapter because they really deserve a section all to themselves. So stick with me . . . read on!

6

Do-It-Yourself Doctoring

There is an old saying among medical men that "the doctor who treats himself has a fool for a patient." But not, I venture to suggest, if he is diabetic. The fact is that, more than with any other condition I know of, the diabetic simply has to understand the nature of the illness and become intimately involved in treating it. In the life of diabetics, ignorance is not bliss. This treatment regime has been compared to a three-legged stool. The proper balance I have been talking about is the seat on which you are supported. The three legs are insulin (or pills), diet, and exercise. Now, like a stool, the program to maintain control will not function if one of these props is missing or faulty. It is no good trying to regulate your blood sugar levels with insulin if you are frantically bingeing on fiberless carbohydrates throughout the day. Nor is it any use trying to keep healthy without a fair amount of regular exercise, which does not, by the way, mean violent overexertion in the cause of "fitness," as I'll explain later.

In this chapter I want to concentrate on the aspect of diabetes that I for one found frightening in the early days: the need for daily insulin injections. Before I do, though, let me explain why in my case insulin was prescribed while a lot of other diabetics maintain themselves in a state of balance on pills.

The basic difference between the pill takers and the

43

insulin injectors lies in the severity of their diabetes. Diabetes can take a number of forms, as I have said, and does not always result from a complete breakdown of insulin production in the pancreas. I was unlucky in that, in middle age, I contracted a severe form of diabetes that necessitated a permanent association with insulin. Most people in my age group, however, are able to control their blood sugar levels with careful diet and exercise. If this fails, then pills can supplement the regime by helping the pancreas to release more insulin or by helping the insulin produced naturally to do its job of sugar breakdown more efficiently. Learning about diabetes and its effects on *me* has brought me into contact with the experiences of many other sufferers, a lot of whom never use insulin but rely instead on pills. So for those of you faced with the prospect of pill-popping, here are a few guidelines to help you on your way.

Presently there are four types of pills available for diabetics in the United States. Called *sulfonylureas*, they are as follows:

Chemical Name	Trade Name
acetohexamide	Dymelor
chlorpropamide	Diabinese
tolazamide	Tolinase
tolbutamide	Orinase

Sulfa drugs have been used for some time to treat all kinds of infections, but it was subsequently discovered about thirty years ago that their *derivatives* had an effect on blood sugar. What appears to happen (though it is not yet clear how) is that the sulfonylureas stimulate the pancreas to secrete more insulin than it would normally. They don't persuade a pancreas totally incapable of generating the hormone to do so. They merely increase a flagging output.

Sulfonylureas are used to supplement a regime of control by diet (not to replace it) and will not be effective as a substitute for insulin. Occasionally a lean, adult diabetic with a closely controlled diet has been known to move onto these oral hypoglycemic pills after being on insulin. The same is true for some overweight diabetics who are managing to shed excess fat without difficulty.

The various pills listed above vary in several respects: strength of dose, duration of action, and side effects. Tolbutamide, for example, is short-acting, needing to be taken more than once a day, while chlorpropamide is long-acting. The more pills you take, of whatever kind, the more these will lower blood sugar, although there is an upper limit of effectiveness to these pills. Hypoglycemic reactions are uncommon, but they can occur. Sometimes other drugs, such as aspirin, will react with sulfonylureas to increase the strength of their action, producing an inadvertent overdose. So be careful not to mix drugs. And keep in close touch with your doctor.

Another danger is from side effects. If you experience any unusual symptoms, such as a high temperature, rashes, sore throat, or tiredness, see your doctor immediately. The same is true of apparently minor gastric upsets, nausea, and headaches. Watch, too, the effects of alcohol. This can also cause unpleasant reactions.

You may, if you are taking any of these antidiabetes pills, have heard the occasional horror story about fatal long-term side effects such as heart attacks—as if you didn't already have enough to worry about! Well, a research study carried out in the United States suggested that these drugs might increase your chances of a coronary. But the evidence is not clear-cut and has not been for more than a decade. So doctors are confident about continuing to prescribe these drugs on the grounds that the undeniable benefits outweigh the unconfirmed risks.

But there are risks and risks. All sulfonylureas lower blood sugar, so if you are taking them, never be without a sugary snack ready to hand in case you miss a meal or are exercising strenuously. Remember, never go without your sugar supply.

Few phrases can be as widely abused as the terms *miracle cure* or *wonder drug*. The fault, dear Brutus, lies not only in the hands of copy editors on popular newspapers and magazines, but in ourselves. We want—need—to believe in medicine as having magical powers. Yet the doctors and medical researchers who work to discover the drugs we label as "miraculous" are usually far less euphoric than we are about their brainchildren. They know their limitations and, anyway, as scientists they are trained not to believe in miracles. However, if there is one exception to this rule, one drug that even doctors talk about in almost reverentially respectful terms, that substance is insulin. Insulin saves lives—not just improves their quality, but saves them, millions of them. It can triumph over an illness that otherwise would kill with the certainty of an advanced cancer. It dramatically, overnight, turns near-invalids into whole persons and maintains them for as long as they like in a physical condition that allows them to do anything. I know, because it has done as much for me, and any diabetics who turn their backs on a miracle such as this are damn fools.

When you are as dependent on a drug as many diabetics are on insulin, you feel almost as if you are developing a "relationship" with it. It becomes a friend. And you want, as you would with any friend, to know a lot more about it. In fact you feel you need to understand how it works if the relationship is to continue to be a happy one. So I make no apology for what follows—a short overview of a remarkable substance: "Everything you always wanted to know about the hormone but have not yet been able to ask."

Sources

I suppose I ought to start by reminding you how much insulin-dependent diabetics (who amount to about a sixth of all sufferers) owe to our four-legged friends the cow and the pig. Commercially, the chief source of the hormone is from the pancreas of slaughtered animals. Synthetic versions also exist—and I'll be going into those later when I discuss research—but are nowhere near as useful yet as the naturally occurring substances. Although both cattle and pig preparations are effective, there are slight chemical differences between the two, which is why it is advisable to stick to one or the other, if it has worked for you. On rare occasions it is possible to develop an allergy to one type or the other. Pure pork insulin is less likely than beef to produce allergic side effects.

Who Needs Insulin?

The simple answer is this: those who cannot produce it for themselves or, if they can, not in sufficient quantity to be effective as a regulator of blood sugar levels. Those diabetics who naturally manufacture some—but not much—insulin may be helped not so much with insulin injections as with a controlled diet, with or without the backup of pills. In fact, some diabetics wrongly feel that they *must* have insulin for their condition, which has led some doctors in the United States to notice that a small percentage of adult diabetics inject themselves when they don't really need to. If you are overweight and inactive, some exercise plus a calorie-controlled diet may obviate the need altogether. Some people manage to come off insulin altogether, but you should never attempt to do so without your doctor's advice and consent.

Who, then, are the long-term insulin candidates? Here's the opinion of Dr. James W. Anderson, Professor of Medicine and Clinical Nutrition at the University of Kentucky and an experienced, active professional in the field of diabetes research and treatment:

> You will probably always need insulin if: you were started on it before you were thirty years old; you are very lean or skinny and take over thirty units of insulin a day; if you are very lean and exercise a great deal (for example, run 15 miles [24 km] a week or briskly walk 3 miles [5 km] a day) and take over twenty units a day.

Yet another category of insulin takers, temporarily at least, are those diabetics on a diet-plus-pills regime who develop an infection or who need to have a surgical operation. Pregnancy, too, may necessitate a temporary switch, again strictly under your doctor's supervision, please.

Types of Insulin

We can classify insulin in a variety of ways, namely:

source ("beef" or "pork" flavor)
length of action
purity
strength

The choice of insulin made by your doctor will be influenced by all these factors. We have already discussed the animal source. Next comes duration of action. Of the many different types of insulin commercially available in the United States, all but the *regular or soluble insulins* have an extended duration of action, beginning to take effect two to three hours after subcutaneous administration, reaching a peak after eight hours or so, and lasting sixteen to twenty-four hours. In *NPH* and *protamine zinc insulins*, the action of the insulin is extended by binding the insulin molecule to a substance called *protamine*. In the Lente group of insulins, an extended time effect is achieved by varying the crystalline size. These insulins are cloudy.

In recent years, commercial insulins have been prepared in a purified form. This means that they have less contamination by the protein proinsulin. Conventional USP (generic) insulin generally has a purity of greater than 10,000 parts per million (ppm) of proinsulin to insulin. "Improved single peak" insulin, which was first marketed in 1980, has less than 50 ppm proinsulin, and "purified" insulins have less than 10 parts per million of proinsulin. Most physicians feel that the purified insulins are not necessary for most patients with uncomplicated diabetes. However, they seem to have a number of advantages over other insulins, namely that they produce fewer "insulin antibodies"—blood proteins to protect the body from the "invasion" of the foreign animal tissue; they make for fewer irritations and red patches at injection sites; they can be taken in smaller doses; they are less likely to produce an allergic response, which is particularly useful if the insulin is being taken temporarily, such as during pregnancy, and may be needed again in later years. As the price differential narrows, more patients will be switched to the purer products.

Insulin Cocktails

Sometimes your doctor may suggest that you combine two of the above types of insulin for better effect. He may, for example, think that there are advantages in mixing a fast-acting soluble insulin with a slower-acting NPH or Lente suspension, putting these two substances together in the correct proportions in the syringe before you inject. Follow his advice to the letter on this because some insulins do not mix well with others. If you are unsure or unwilling over the whole subject, there are ready-mixed preparations available. If you do prefer to mix your own, make sure you have the correct proportions. A trick I have used is to draw into the syringe the two insulins always in the same order—the regular first: that way I know I am not going to mix 3 to 1 when it should be 1 to 3.

Insulin Strength

"Strength" of insulin is measured in units per milliliter. In the United States the standard strength of insulin is 100 units per milliliter—U-100, with the weaker U-40 and U-80 falling out of use. Variations exist, however. Special

INSULINS CURRENTLY AVAILABLE IN THE UNITED STATES

Species Source/ Purity/ Type of Action	Lilly Products	Novo Products	Nordisk Products	Squibb Products
Pork (Purified, <10 ppm)	Iletin II Pork			
Rapid-acting	Regular	Actrapid (Regular)	Quick (regular) (Velosulin®)	
		Semitard (Semilente)	Mixtard*	
Intermediate- acting	NPH Lente	Monotard (Lente)	NPH (Insulatard®)	
Long-acting	PZI			

Species Source/ Purity/ Type of Action	Lilly Products	Novo Products	Nordisk Products	Squibb Products
Beef (Purified,				
< 10 ppm)	Iletin II Beef			
Rapid-acting	Regular			
Intermediate-	NPH			
acting	Lente			
Long-acting	PZI	Ultratard (Ultralente)		
Beef-Pork (Purified, < 10 ppm)				
Intermediate-acting		Lentard (Lente)		
Beef-Pork (USP, Improved Single Peak, < 50 ppm)	Iletin I			
Rapid-acting	Regular Semilente			
Intermediate-	NPH			
acting	Lente			
Long-acting	PZI Ultralente			
Beef-Pork (USP, Conventional, > 10,000 ppm)				
Rapid-acting				Regular
Intermediate-				NPH
acting				Globin
Long-acting				PZI
Beef (USP, Conventional, > 10,000 ppm)				
Rapid-acting				Semilente
Intermediate-				Lente
acting				
Long-acting				Ultralente

*Mixture of 30% regular and 70% NPH. (Data provided by Eli Lilly and Company, Indianapolis, Indiana 46285.)

needs are served by U-500 and other strengths. To ensure that you inject the correct dosage of insulin, the different strengths need appropriately calibrated syringes so that you can see at a glance how many units you have drawn up.

Dosages

As my diabetes is of the juvenile type, I have to inject myself twice a day: seven days a week, fifty-two weeks in the year. The correct dosage and mixtures have been worked out for me by my doctors, and I'm assuming that you, like me, accept that this is the only sensible way to arrive at the proper drug therapeutic program. But diabetes is not one of those conditions where you just go on taking the medicine unfailingly and unquestioningly, year in, year out. The human body is not an automobile or an electric blender that reacts mechanically to the demands put on it. Particularly for the diabetic, whose condition touches on every aspect of the body's functioning, it soon becomes clear that variations occur that only he or she is close enough to detect. And when they do, the fixed doses may need to be adjusted.

To have diabetes means to me not only having a condition about which I constantly learn new facts, but also having a hand in my own everyday well-being. If, for example, I find that I have a high urine sugar level before lunch several days in a row, despite my pre-breakfast injection, I consult with my doctor and we work out a way of combating this that involves increasing the insulin amount by, say, two units. Conversely I may find that at the same time of day I have a hypoglycemic reaction, as if the dosage earlier had been too high. So we (my doctor and I) again work out a slight change of dosage. Only my doctor can tell me just how big an increase or decrease in insulin is safe for me. But he needs my knowledge of how my body is functioning to reach his decision.

Dosage, then, is not invariable. It may need fine adjustments to match the demands or lack of demand your body is putting on the insulin you have given it. It may be that one day in the week at a fixed time you indulge in some violent exercise such as squash or rowing. Could it be that a smaller dose of insulin is called for that day because you are lowering your blood sugar by another means? Think about your daily and weekly routines, and about those unexpected times when they are disrupted (which happens to me a lot) and see whether your urine analysis suggests some modifications to your insulin dose.

Problems with Insulin

Problems can occur. In fact there is no such thing as a drug totally without side effects, which vary according to the individual. When I began to inject myself I felt some stinging pains around the injection sites, but these soon disappeared. Other diabetics have told me that in the first few weeks they found blotchy red swellings, which again passed.

More serious are local infections, which may occur if needles and syringes are not kept scrupulously clean. Allergy to insulin may also develop, with hives or itchy skin patches. Delayed allergic reactions often disappear by themselves, while immediate allergic reactions may be helped by switching to a purified pork insulin. Another source of local allergy is not the insulin itself but the skin cleansing solution. If this seems to be the case, your doctor will be able to help you around this particular problem.

Another problem is insulin resistance. Some people

are simply not as responsive as others to the hormone, or, rather, their bodies possess a more rugged defense system in the form of antibodies than the rest of us. This may lead to a dosage as high as 200 units a day or more, and a need to switch to a highly purified form of pork insulin.

Some months after beginning insulin injections, yet another problem may arise in the mechanisms regulating body fat. You may notice that in the areas of the thigh or buttock where you have been injecting yourself the subcutaneous fat begins to melt away, leaving unsightly hollows. This *fat atrophy*, as it's called, is not dangerous, but neither is it something anyone would like to live with. Although there is no specific treatment, certain measures may be helpful. Your doctor may recommend switching sites constantly so that each local area (one-inch square) is not used more than once every three to four weeks. Or direct intravenous injection into the atrophied area may be recommended. Using room-temperature insulin may help. The opposite condition of *fat hypertrophy* can also occur— more rarely, it should be stressed—in which you get unwanted mounds of fat at your injection sites. The trick here is, again, to vary the sites, which means using a little imagination.

Sites for Sore Thighs

First let me say that other diabetics, more than any doctor, have helped me discover places to inject myself. And I've thought about the problem a lot myself.

You take a course in school, then you leave school and you start applying it, using your imagination, enlarging on what you've learned. When I started out as a diabetic, I made the amazing discovery that although when you're giving yourself an injection in the morning you think you're going to remember in the evening where you gave it, by seven at night, when you sit down to give yourself your shot, you can't remember where the hell you put the needle in that morning. So my husband used to draw a body and put the date on a certain position like sticking tails on a donkey or flags in a map. And I'd say, "Oops, I did it on my left thigh this morning because my chart tells me that, so I'll go to the other side." But during the last year I have stopped using the chart because I instinctively change my spot—I can't explain why. I don't even think about it.

I have never injected in my arm because I physically can't do it. Another reason is that I'm thin and don't have much flesh there. I just hate the idea of injecting in my arm, and on a woman it shows in sleeveless dresses. Which leaves me with the thighs, and now that miniskirts are on the way back I could be in real trouble, but then there's always my backside. I'm very agile. I can get way back on my backside, right on my hip where it's a little fleshier.

A very nice man named Brian Jones who's with a London advertising agency, and is also diabetic, once told me that under my bosom was a good spot, with plenty of fatty tissue but very few veins. I ran home, all excited, to try this new place, got the needle out and drew it up, sitting on the side of the bed, about 7:30 P.M., and looked down to inject myself. Now I am, as they say, fairly generously endowed (I wear a 36C-cup bra) and I couldn't see this place he'd told me about. So I got to laughing and I called his house and spoke to his wife and said, "Where is Brian?" I couldn't resist the temptation. She said he was at the tennis club, so I called him there, got him off the court, and said, "Thanks a lot, Brian. You know that new spiffy spot you told me about? Well, in my case I can't see the forest for the trees, if you know what I mean?" He got a big kick out of my dilemma, and what's more I finally found a way to focus under the 36C cup. Quite an achievement!

The injection sites you choose may also, to some extent, be influenced by your life-style. Some researchers at Yale University studied the effectiveness of insulin injection on diabetics who were given athletic exercises to do involving a lot of leg work. They injected their subjects in the leg, arm, and abdomen and found that leg "jabbers" who ran or bicycled were more apt to develop hypoglycemia than arm "jabbers." The converse was true for those who used their arms in exercise. Exercise of an extremity increases the rate of mobilization of insulin. Therefore if you use your legs a great deal, jab elsewhere. And if you're an inveterate arm swinger, inject in the legs or thighs!

Normally insulin injections are made under the skin, with great care taken to avoid any veins. However, it may be that direct intravenous injections may be helpful if you are unfortunate enough to need a sudden massive insulin dose when things have got wildly out of control. Doctors at London's Royal Free Hospital experimented with direct injections of insulin into the bloodstream. This is not an easy thing to do, because an ordinary syringe injection would be unsuitable. So the insulin has to be added to a suitable liquid such as a saline solution, and then this is dripped into a vein at a carefully controlled rate. It transpired that one particular patient needing a colossal tally of 3,000 units a day could be reduced to 50 units, with better control of the diabetes, when the insulin was led directly into a vein.

Injection Sites

Think of the body as seven or eight regions and inject in one region for a week before moving to the next. These are the eight: right thigh; left thigh; right buttock; left buttock; right upper arm; left upper arm; abdomen; under breasts

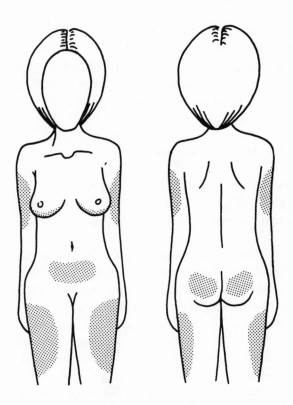

(for women). Omit any of these you feel unhappy about, *but stick to your rotational order.*

As a rule, though, for subcutaneous injections, the secret is to vary your sites in a strict rotation, like a farmer moving his crops around from season to season. In your case a season is about a week, the field is a theoretical area marked out on your body (see my pin-a-tail style diagram), and the spacing of the crops—or needle entry points—not less than one inch (2.5 cm) apart.

Injection Procedures

If you are new to the business of injecting yourself, here are the steps you will have to learn for successful self-therapy. They will soon become indelibly imprinted on your memory. If you're an old hand, you may find something of use anyway, just to make life easier, and safer.

How to Inject Yourself

Always use the correct syringes and needles your doctor has prescribed for you. In Britain most people tend to use nondisposable syringes (the British Standard 1619), which are specially made for insulin, with the correct marking on the side (20 marks per milliliter). If a nondisposable needle is used, this can be kept with the syringe in the case, which contains alcohol, a sterile fluid that must be changed when it goes cloudy. Keep a spare syringe and needle in case of breakage. And change the needle when it gets blunt.

In the United States, Canada, Australia, and South Africa disposable syringes are practically universal. Again, the markings are just right for insulin administration. One mark equals one unit, 100 marks per milliliter.

Disposable needles can also be used with ordinary nondisposable syringes. They may last up to one week.

One final word on injections: as I said earlier, I was horrified at the whole idea of sticking a needle into myself, but I very quickly began to take what almost amounts to a professional pride in doing the job quickly and efficiently, so that it does not interfere with the more interesting business of living a normal life. And besides, I found that it's even possible to use all the paraphernalia of insulin-dependence to make life a little more colorful.

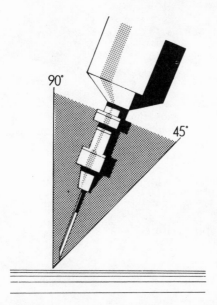

When I don't like something I make a one-act play out of it. I thought: I'm going to have some fun out of this diabetes, and inject, if you'll pardon the pun, a little humor as well as insulin. The first time I went to America after I developed diabetes, I was there for six weeks. That's forty-five days, which means 90 syringes, 90 extra needles, 90 medi-swabs, and about 3 bottles of insulin. I always take much more insulin than I'm going to use because those bottles could break and the kind of insulin I was using at the time you actually cannot get in America. Anyway, there it was in my makeup case: 90 syringes, 90 needles, and 90 medi-swabs and all these little bottles. I arrived at the U.S. customs and there, glowering at me, was this customs woman. She tipped the scale at about 200 pounds and looked like every filmmaker's idea of a guard in a women's prison. She even had a bunch of keys

Drawing Insulin

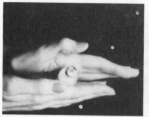

1. After first thoroughly washing your hands, mix insulin completely by gently rolling bottle between your hands. Never shake the insulin.

2. Clean the top of the insulin bottle with an alcohol swab.

3. Draw same amount of air into syringe as the insulin dose you require.

4. With the bottle upright, insert needle into rubber stopper and push plunger down.

5. Turn the bottle and syringe upside down. Slowly draw up slightly more insulin than your dose.

6. If there are any air bubbles in the syringe, flick or tap at the bubble. When it goes to the top of the syringe, push the plunger until the bubble goes into the bottle. Draw your exact dose again.

Injecting Insulin

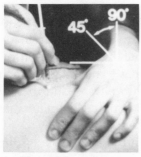

1. Clean skin with alcohol and let dry. Grasp same area between your thumb and fingers, raising skin and fat away from muscle. Hold syringe as shown and inject needle quickly into skin at an angle of 45 to 90 degrees.

2. Release skin. Pull back plunger about 2 or 3 units. Make sure there is no blood in syringe. If there is blood, *don't inject*, as it means the needle is in a blood vessel. Throw syringe away and start again.

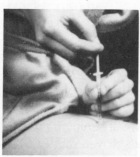

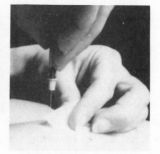

3. Push plunger down quickly and steadily in 3 to 5 seconds.

4. Quickly pull needle from the skin and gently hold an alcohol swab on the injection site to close opening left by needle. Don't massage area.

dangling around her waist, like she was locking people up in the morning before she came to work. I heard her before I got up to her and she was really being tough on people. "Open everything!" and "What's your mother's maiden name?", putting everybody through it—and there was a line you wouldn't believe. So I thought I'd put her on a bit, or as they say in Britain, "take the mickey."

I weighed under 125 pounds and had a smashing fur coat on, good makeup, and very sexy high-heeled shoes, which I rarely wear. Anyway, I opened my case containing the medical kit quite blatantly and there were all these needles and things. It was such a wonderful thing to watch the expression on her face. She could have thought many things. She could've thought I was on narcotics or something. She said, "Well, what about this?" and I said, "What about what? You don't like it any more than I do, it's a pain in the neck." I just kept leading her up the garden path and she kept saying, "Can you explain this?" and I said, "Yes, if you've got a few days to give me your undivided attention."

She said, "I just think . . . I just think . . ." She didn't know what to say.

"I don't," I said, "want to bore you with all the details of this, you know, how many injections I do a day, or why, or the story of my life [really enjoying it now] . . . what's led me to this and what's driven me."

She just couldn't get her mouth closed, so finally she said, "I am . . . I think I'd better get my . . . my superintendent." I began to feel a little bit guilty about it all, and then out comes another woman who looks like she could have thrown my husband over a customs barrier. "What seems to be the trouble?" And there I was standing with my card that says I'M A DIABETIC. Of course she looks at this woman and says, "What's all this fuss about?" The first woman replied blankly, "Well, she didn't . . ." It was a bit of a dirty trick on my part, but it was warranted, really—you'd agree if you could have seen this woman and how she was behaving with people.

Anyway I waltzed through customs feeling a bit guilty for taking advantage of one of those less fortunate than I am. What I'm saying is: I'm the one with diabetes, but she's the one with a nasty disposition. I think I'm ahead. Something I've done all my life is to try to see the humor in every situation and use it, because it's the best medicine in the world. I'm not saying it's easy to do, but I think it's good for all of us to realize that it's possible to look at the bright side, the positive side, or whatever.

Oh, by the way, if you are traveling on a plane or train or boat, don't think that you have immediately to seek out the nearest refrigerator to store your current requirement of insulin. It is as comfortable as you are in normal room temperatures. Keep the drug cool, though, for longer-term use. And never attempt to use it when the expiration date on the box has passed.

Now, what was I on about? Oh yes, keep laughing. Believe me, it helps.

7

Exchange Is No Robbery

Can there be anything more boring—or more time-consuming—than the person who is constantly "watching what she eats," like some overzealous Mother Hen, tirelessly weighing every tiniest morsel that passes the lips, in case (the unforgivable sin!) "too much" of the "wrong sort of food" should creep into the unsuspecting digestive system and/or make her fat! Well, that's never been me, and it is not me now that I am a diabetic. Food is to be eaten and enjoyed but not, in any sense other than the literal, made a meal of.

There are a few rules, or guidelines if you prefer, that I have decided are necessary. Not enough to turn me or you into a crashing diet bore, but sufficient to ensure that the good effects of regular insulin injections, coupled with daily exercise (more about that later), are not dissipated by a head-in-the-sand attitude to food consumption. Actually, a few basic rules are a good idea, whether you are a diabetic or not. In my prediabetes days I have to admit I was an irregular eat-anything, eat-anytime sort of person. I would almost always skip breakfast altogether, grab a light, hurried, ill-assembled lunch, then, in the evening, usually after a performance—12:30 or 1 A.M.—eat everything in sight. You don't need a degree in Applied Nutrition to recognize the folly in that sort of life-style.

So rule one is: think about that much-used term *a*

balanced diet and make sure that what you eat throughout the day is just that. Don't load one part of the day with one type of food, and another part with something different. To follow this prescription means, inevitably, knowing something about the composition of everyday foods and what they supply as essential nourishment. To help you, I've put together a few simple checklists, to which you can refer from time to time. There is also a comprehensive table printed in the Appendix for checking against in greater detail.

Food is fuel, providing the body with the materials for sustaining its growth and repair as well as the energy for keeping all the physiological processes going. It consists of a mixture of carbohydrates, protein, fat, vitamins, and minerals, in varying proportions according to the sort of meal you put together.

CARBOHYDRATES are principally an energy source, found mainly in plant foods, and they can be divided into two groups:

> Sugars, especially sucrose, found in brown or white sugar, cakes, jams, sweets; lactose, found in milk; and fructose, found in fruit and vegetables.
>
> Starches, found in wheat, oats, flour, bread, barley, rice, pasta, cereals, cornmeal, potatoes, fruit, and green vegetables.

Both starches and sugars, once eaten, get converted into glucose, which is, as we know, the diabetic's potential enemy. Too many carbohydrates and not enough insulin, and you end up with high blood sugar. Too many carbohydrates (or calories) and sufficient insulin, and you end up with an excess of fat tissue. Foods containing simple carbohydrates (sugary foods such as cakes and cookies) should be limited in the diet, as they cause a sharp rise in blood sugar and have a low nutrient-to-calorie ratio.

PROTEINS   are the body builders par excellence. You get these in meats, poultry, fish, dairy produce such as cheese, eggs, and a number of plant foods such as nuts and beans. A balanced protein intake means eating food containing both animal- and vegetable-derived forms of these vital substances. For a diabetic, all meals and snacks should contain a protein source so that insulin can be used over a longer period of time. Also, protein has a high satiety value; that is, it makes you feel fuller for a longer period of time than carbohydrates.

FATS   are where the calories are, so they are to be watched carefully if you are a diabetic prone to put on weight. It has been estimated that we need a minimum of 5 grams of fat a day. I'd like to bet that most people (and this is undoubtedly true in the United States) get through at least ten times that amount. Fats are everywhere, in most animal or plant foods but only in relatively small amounts in vegetables and fruit. Go easy on the butter, cream, cooking and salad oils, and so on. And remember that most meat contains so-called *saturated fats*—a source of high blood cholesterol.

VITAMINS   are essential and can be obtained from foods without the need for vitamin pills unless you tend for some reason or another (perhaps economic necessity) to take in a very repetitive, restricted diet. We need about thirteen different vitamins from a wide variety of foods. I won't go through the vitamin alphabet here to show you where you can get A, B, C, etc.; I'll merely remind you that you'll get all you need from green vegetables, fruits, meat, fish, poultry, eggs, cereals, and bread.

The same applies to *minerals*. We need about a dozen of these chemicals to keep the bodily machine running smoothly, again from a variety of foods. Some are so-called *trace minerals*, which again we should have no difficulty in obtaining in the normal course of eating. Deficiencies in minerals are not unknown, but if these occur, you should talk to your doctor.

Before I go on to the practicalities of eating as a diabetic, there is one topic I really must touch on here, because it has repeatedly cropped up in conversations I have had with fellow diabetics: *dietary fiber*. This substance, also known as roughage, is really the outer protective husk of plants. It is well known as an aid to regular bowel movements and in recent years has acquired a reputation for staving off various internal complaints, such as diverticulitis. Many people have begun to look on fiber almost as a magical supplement to their diet. I won't go as far as that, but I will tell you about an interesting research project carried out by Dr. David Jenkins at Oxford University, England. Dr. Jenkins focused his investigation on a jelly-like substance called guar that is extracted from the cluster bean, grown in India and elsewhere as a foodstuff. The guar comes from the fibrous cell walls of the bean, though it is not strictly speaking a fiber product itself. Dr. Jenkins wondered whether the now widespread belief in fiber as being medicinally helpful might extend to the diabetic, so he donned his chef's apron and began to make bread and marmalade with high concentrations of guar and another cell-wall jelly-like substance, pectin. These foods were then fed to diabetics.

The rate at which the subjects' blood sugar levels rose after a meal was measured alongside that of a control group of diabetics not fed guar and pectin. Apparently the "fiber" group, if I can call them that, had a slower rise in blood sugar levels, suggesting that they were absorbing sugar more gradually from the intestines into the bloodstream. The implications were clear. Such a diet could put less strain on the pancreas and lower the demands on a diabetic's already deficient insulin-supply mechanism. Further research, using guar, seems to have confirmed the early promising results. A guar-reinforced diet appears to help the more mild diabetic to enjoy an otherwise normal life without the need for insulin injections. It may also help the more serious diabetic, too, by reducing the chances of secondary damage to the eyes, kidneys, heart, and nervous system.

Even more recently, researchers have found out that you do not need guar-type fiber to produce results. You can also get your fiber from the more familiar wheat bran, found in wholemeal bread. But you may have noticed something of a paradox here. In fact, I can hear some of you saying to yourselves, "Okay, a high-fiber diet will slow down the rise in blood sugar levels, but fiber is found in many different foods that contain carbohydrates. And carbohydrates are my main worry." Well, that's true, but there are carbohydrates and carbohydrates. You must still watch the cakes, cookies, and desserts because they don't give you any roughage anyway. But you can tolerate more carbohydrates from fiber-rich vegetables, beans, wholemeal bread, cereals, and other starchy foods, far more perhaps than in your usual carbohydrate-restricted diet. I admit this is a bit confusing, but the evidence does seem to be that "all carbohydrates are dangerous but some are more dangerous than others. And some are useful!" Remember that there is also fiber and fiber. According to Dr. Jim Mann, member of the British Diabetic Association Nutrition Sub-Committee, there are two main types of dietary fiber:

> "Fibrous" fibres typically found in bran, wholegrain cereals or wholemeal flour and "viscous" fibres found in pulses (peas, beans and lentils) and some fruits and vegeta-

bles. Viscous fibres (especially those found in beans) appear to be of particular benefit to the diabetic because they retard food absorption and hence slow down the rate at which carbohydrate present in a meal will be absorbed into the bloodstream.

All plant foods, especially those which are raw or only lightly cooked, are digested at a very slow rate owing to the plant cell walls which have to be broken down before the carbohydrate contained within them is released.

While we're on the topic of confusing diabetic diets, you may care to know that we diabetics are besieged with a lot of highly variegated advice. Three British experts in the early 1970s carried out a survey of the dietary policies and management practices in hundreds of diabetic clinics in the United Kingdom. They found, when they'd put together all the replies from doctors dishing out advice to diabetics, that there is ''uncertainty about the ideal dietary policy for diabetics.'' Even more so, there are real variations in the way it is explained. Many of the diet sheets were contradictory and difficult to follow (but things have improved since then). Which brings me to my second rule: don't be too bogged down by what I call the ''technicalities'' of eating. Be sensible, not obsessive.

Now to the practicalities. Let's assume for a moment that being overweight is not a problem. (We'll come to that later when we look at calories.) The real preoccupation for you is to know how many carbohydrates you are allowed—which your doctor will tell you (100 grams? 150? 200?)—then:

How are these to be made up?

Which foods are carbohydrate free?

How can I get variety?

Well, the answers to all these questions can be derived from the same exercise; namely, one of exchanges. You need to have a complete carbohydrate list in a form you can use for calculating intake. There are a variety of books available in paperback that give everyday foods with their calorie and carbohydrate content. For a complete reference, you can use *Food Values of Portions Commonly Used*, thirteenth edition, by Jean Pennington and Helen N. Church (Harper & Row trade paperback, 1980). Or again, you can refer to the list in the Appendix, which is from the American Diabetes Association. I suggest you start to build up your own list, with the foods you tend to eat, the ideal ultimately being that you have your own tailor-made countdown for easy reference.

I think perhaps we ought just to take stock at this point and look at the basic rules for successful diabetic eating. Let's go back to the experts, to Dr. Jim Mann, who sums up the British Diabetic Association's recommendations as follows:

1. Excessive energy content (be it from any source like protein, fat and carbohydrate) in the diet worsens diabetic control. Therefore each patient requires a diet which does not contain a surplus amount of food energy and must be based on individual need.

2. The proportion of fat in the diet should be reduced to lessen the risk from coronary heart and arterial disease. In practical terms this means: using skimmed milk instead of whole milk in cooking; using a low-fat spread instead of butter or margarine; grilling [broiling] rather than frying food; eating chicken, turkey, and fish rather than beef, lamb, pork and manufactured meat products; greatly reducing intake of cheese (except cottage and curd cheese), cream and visible fat on meat.

3. Provided the fat intake is reduced, carbohydrate intake can be increased to meet the energy needs of the diabetic, which should be individually determined. The type of carbohydrate eaten is important. Diabetics should continue to avoid rapidly-absorbed carbohydrate such as

sugar and sugary foods but should eat more of the slowly-absorbed foods, rich in fibre. The diabetic should: eat more fruit, vegetables and beans; eat wholemeal [whole wheat] bread instead of white; use wholemeal flour for baking instead of white; use brown rice or spaghetti instead of their refined equivalents; eat a high-fibre breakfast cereal such as shredded wheat, All-Bran or unsweetened muesli instead of cereals such as corn flakes or Rice Krispies.

4.   Because of the need for balance between carbohydrate intake and injected insulin (or anti-diabetic tablet treatment) the distribution and timing of carbohydrate eaten during the day remains crucial.

5.   *It is no longer considered that the diabetic who needs to lose weight should follow a diet low in carbohydrate* [my italics—ES]. The high carbohydrate, low fat diet now recommended for all diabetics is particularly suitable for those who are overweight because it is a bulky diet and hence less likely to cause hunger.

6.   In view of the possible links between salt (sodium) intake and raised blood pressure (which contributes to arterial disease), diabetics should not consume a diet which contains more salt than that of the non-diabetic.

7.   The use of special diabetic foods is not encouraged because these products are expensive and of little health benefit. However, low-calorie foods and drinks can be useful especially for the diabetics who need to lose weight. Saccharine and aspartame (a new artificial sweetener) are acceptable substitutes for sugar.

8.   Unless contrary to medical advice, diabetics may have moderate amounts of alcohol provided that its energy contribution is taken into account. Beers and lagers specially brewed for diabetics are not essential and their relatively high alcohol and energy content necessitates cautious use.

When I was in the hospital, I paid very close attention to the menu, learning as I went along from experience, the

same attitude I have when doing a play. In fact the most
enjoyable way for me to do anything is to pick it up as I go
along rather than make a big piece out of it. When I'm in
the theater I never have any trouble learning lines because
you rehearse for four or five weeks and it just goes in. In an
interesting way, this is the opposite of what I used to do in
school as a kid: I used to cram for an exam and get it on
paper and win first prize because I had a miraculously
retentive memory. Anyway, what I did in the hospital was
to see how many potatoes were there, and check off my list
and ask for ten carbohydrates' worth of potatoes and ten
carbohydrates' worth of carrots and the rest in my dessert.
So I utilized my time in the hospital trying to simplify it all.
The result was that I've never used kitchen scales for my
"diabetic diet" because for me it makes it so unattractive.
I just cannot. I follow my instinct too strongly; it has
always played a very important part in my life and I've
been about 98 percent right most of the time. I haven't
always acted on instinct, but when I do, I very rarely let
myself down.

The plain truth is that I do not intend to spend the rest
of my life weighing carrots. It's not in me to do it and I just
refuse to do it. By this I don't mean to give anyone the
impression that you can, if your list says "One slice of thin
toast," cut two pieces of bread an inch thick and say you
had twenty carbohydrates for breakfast. That's just silly.
It's like people who have a drink at home, pouring a
gigantic shot of booze and then saying they had "a" drink
before dinner. They did not have "a" drink before dinner.
They had "four" drinks before dinner in one glass.
They're kidding themselves, and they know it.

So it's up to you, kid, to make up your mind whether
you're going to fool yourself to death or tell yourself the
truth to live! But I have got along pretty well, without
being a slave to a diet. I eat a lot of stewed fruit, and one
day in the hospital they brought in my twenty carbohy-

drates' worth of fruit for dessert, which, with my container of yogurt, would make it thirty. Eight prunes came in dry as a bone, the most unappetizing-looking affair I've ever seen in my life, just eight prunes in a white dish with no juice. So I called the dietician the next morning and said, "Hey, what's with the prunes with no juice?"

She said to me, "Oh, the juice counts." That's a fact, but okay, I'd rather have three prunes with a little juice than four without. Maybe I spill over a little sometimes and sometimes I'm a little under, but I leave it to my instinct and I really get along very well. As I say, you have to be perfectly honest with yourself, because you're not fooling anybody but yourself. However, if maybe you were allowed 150 carbohydrates a day and you go to bed at night having had 168, I don't think they're going to bury you in the morning. . . . I think some diabetics have a tendency to be overly zealous about what they do to live with diabetes. I must admit I am one of them. This, of course, is better than the other extreme, like not giving a hoot in hell about the rules. But try not to feel you've lost the battle because you eat eleven carbohydrates at teatime instead of ten. I think you ought to go easy on yourself, not too easy, but easy.

Another pitfall to avoid is the idea that a diabetic diet is "samey." When you think about it, people do eat more or less the same thing every day. There may be a few galloping gourmets around town who have broiled pike with white wine sauce and grapes on Monday, then steak with madeira sauce and chopped shallots sprinkled with whatever on Tuesday, cabbage à la heavy cream on Wednesday, and so on. Some people eat that way, but it's usually because of their work—expense-account luncheons—right? A large proportion of people have eggs and bacon or cereal or toast or perhaps a danish for breakfast and they have it every day of their lives.

I often lunch with people who repeat themselves time after time. They get hung up on a green salad and they don't want to put on weight, so they have one every day for lunch. And once in a while they make a switch, which is what I do. For instance sometimes I get terribly sophisticated and do not have my prunes and apricots, but (and this is very rare) switch and have a small potato and an order of carrots, just like a "normal" person sitting there having dinner. Then maybe I'll have four apricots and yogurt for dessert. But that change is not a birthday party to me, I don't look forward to it. I do look forward to my prunes and I don't care who knows it.

A lot of my eating is done in restaurants or hotels, or at friends' homes during lunch or supper parties, and this immediately raises the question of how intrusive your diabetic regime has to be. Suppose, for example, your hostess unknowingly serves something that's off limits to you. What should you do? Nibble nervously and leave most of it, or tell her, even if she is not a bosom buddy and may be offended? There can only be one answer: out with it, carbohydrates included.

I have a sneaking suspicion that one of the biggest worries of most diabetics is the fear of expressing themselves, causing trouble. Even for me, an actress who has worked all her life on not being afraid of people or narrow opinions, even for me it's hard, so I can imagine what it's like for you and you and you. There's the fear of the housewife who's got to feed the family. Is she going to have to do separate things for herself? And so on, and on and on in all our different ways of life. I think the worst four-letter word in the world is "fear," but when you think how precious life is, you should just say "to hell with it" and do your own thing. Whatever it is, so long as you don't do it in the street and frighten the horses, as Mrs. Patrick Campbell once said.

To sum up this business of carbohydrates and the exchange of them: think in terms of 10-gram portions of carbohydrate-containing foods, and divide out as many 10-gram portions as are allowed for your daily intake (15 portions for 150 g/CHO—that's "grams of carbohydrate"—and 20 portions for 200 g/CHO). Use a reference sheet for this.

Space out your carbohydrates throughout the day. Remember, if you take insulin you will need a good amount of carbohydrates at each meal to keep you going throughout the day. You will soon get used to translating 10-gram portions into quantities that make sense: for example, a ⅔-ounce slide of bread equals 10 g/CHO. After a while you'll get like me and leave behind lists of figures. You'll have your reference list and you'll have learned what the equivalent or exchange value of various foods are. If you are completely new to the business of being a carbohydrate-counting fiber-favoring diabetic, here's the sort of daily menu you can put together in that way. Not, I think you'll agree, the fare of a particularly "deprived" individual.

It doesn't take a lot of imagination to see how you can ring the changes on this sort of intake. If you dislike crackers, eat something else with equal CHO value. If you abhor cereal, exchange its carbohydrates for something else, such as fruit, and so on. Personally I've quite enjoyed doing this kind of bartering. It's a bit like playing Monopoly, buying and selling, calculating and weighing up probabilities. But only as a sort of game. Whenever I find myself lapsing into too much mental arithmetic, I check myself and think of something else. But *never* forget you're a diabetic. Never go anywhere without immediate access to carbohydrates. This I learned the hard way in the wilds of Yorkshire.

I went to Yorkshire to visit Russell Harty for ten days.

It was my first vacation for a long time. My husband was in New York, so I telephoned him and said, "Would you mind if I went up to Russell Harty's?"

He said, "Of course not, I think it'll be good for you." (No offence, Russell.) I'd been working extremely hard and the switch of waking up in the morning and having nothing to do was so exciting that I kinda lost my bearings as a diabetic. I took my daily insulin shots, of course, but forgot about the true nature of my condition and what it entailed—discipline-wise. You have a routine (this is something that all diabetics should really think about), and when you change your surroundings be awfully careful and don't change that basic thing. I love to walk, so one day I said to Russell, "Let's get some exercise. Do you like to walk?"

He said, "No." He doesn't mince words, old Russell. Well, it was four miles to the village, so I said, "I'll walk there every morning and you pick me up at the pub. I'll have my little snack of carbohydrates and then we'll have lunch and I'll drive back. Four miles is enough for me."

He said, "Terrific."

I'm always lugging everything about, but now I'm on vacation and I said to Russell, "Why don't I put my little bag into your car and you bring it?" I left the house and started to walk. After a while I looked at my watch. I'd had my shot at nine-thirty, and at eleven-thirty I needed ten carbohydrates. I suddenly thought, "Jesus, Mary, and Joseph, I've left all my stuff in Russell's car." So I'm halfway between the little village and his house and I've got nothing with me. And then when you get nervous about your problem the adrenaline starts working and you can lower your blood sugar even more. I was terrified, I didn't know what to do. Should I go on to the village or back to Russell's house? All that was surrounding me was a lot of sheep going Baa . . . who probably had perfectly healthy pancreases. I got really scared . . . there was nothing, no cars, no farmhouses in the distance. I wondered if I could find a horse. You usually find sugar around a horse—ha ha—I was going a little crazy.

The best thing was to start walking back toward Russell's because then, when I had my hypoglycemic episode, I'd collapse but he'd find me sooner than if I went on to the village. I was panicked. It was twenty to twelve when out of nowhere (and Russell told me that cars hardly ever came up this route) I saw a car coming. I couldn't believe my luck! I got out in the middle of the road, waving and flailing my arms like Medea on a bad day. The car stops. I'm not having a hypo or anything, just anticipating one. I went over and said to the driver, "I'm sorry, sir, to stop you, but do you have anything sweet in your car?"

"No," he said, "I'm traveling alone." A comedian in Yorkshire! "But seriously, young lady," he said, "it's funny you should ask me that." And do you know he was a salesman for Mars Bars and he had a backseat full of candy! Now, that's divine intervention!

"Take anything you want," he said. "How do you feel about peppermint balls?" I was so relieved knowing that I had a candy kitchen on four wheels in front of me. I said, "Now let me see, what will it be?" I opted for the peppermint balls.

He said, "My pleasure," and gave me a bag of the most delicious peppermint balls I've ever tasted in my life. "Would you like a ride into the village?"

I said, "No, all I want in the whole world at this moment are your peppermint balls. . . . You see, sir, I'm diabetic."

And he said, "I don't care, I still think you're a very talented girl!" God, life is funny and wonderful at times, isn't it? Even with diabetes. . . .

SPECIMEN DIET FOR 150 GRAMS CARBOHYDRATE

(15 portions of 10 grams)

	Grams carbohydrate
1 ¼ pints of milk to last the day	30
Breakfast	
One portion cereal (with milk from the allowance)	10
Egg, bacon, fish or cheese	
Two portions bread, toast, or crispbread	20
Tea or coffee	
Midmorning	
Tea or coffee	
Midday meal	
Meat or fish or chicken or cheese or egg as desired	
Two portions of bread or potato or rice	20
Vegetables and salads	
One portion fruit *or*	
Two small plain crackers and cheese	10
Tea or coffee	
Midafternoon	
Two portions bread or plain crackers	20
Tea or coffee	
Evening meal	
Clear soup or grapefruit or melon if desired	
Then as for midday meal	30
Bedtime	
One portion plain cookies	10
Milky drink from remainder of daily allowance	

Total = 150 grams carbohydrate

Note: Butter or margarine can be used as desired. No sugar in tea, coffee, or milky drinks. Saccharin can be added instead.

Source: Life with Diabetes by Dr. Arnold Bloom (British Medical Association). Adapted for U.S. measures.

8
Taking the Weight Off Your Feet

Being overweight for anyone can be uncomfortable and unflattering, to say the least. For an actress it can mean professional suicide—unless, of course, you want to specialize (as some have done with conspicuous success) in well-rounded parts—and the pun is intentional! Funny, isn't it, to think how body fat has in our times become an undesirable attribute? In the Middle Ages, wealth, status, and opulence were thought to be best mirrored by an overfed frame; the more tightly stretched one's clothes over a corpulent waistline, the more one was immediately reckoned to be a Man (or Woman) of Substance, in every sense of the word.

In our relatively affluent times, though, the plain fact is that fatness or obesity is no longer to be courted. It has been recognized for what it is, an unnecessary physical burden that is potentially so harmful as to merit the description of a "disease." Being overweight has dangers for everyone. It overburdens the heart, decreases life expectancy, keeps you feeling constantly breathless, and so on. For the diabetic, though, the dangers of being overweight are even greater. There can be no plainer rule than rule three: don't eat too much of anything. You cannot, must not, be overweight.

Actually, before we look a little at the sorts of food you need to choose to realize that goal—a matter this time not of carbohydrate but of calorie counting—you may be interested in some very intriguing discoveries made by doctors in recent years on this whole question of how body fat seems to relate to diabetes.

A group of researchers at the Medical College of Wisconsin in Milwaukee, under the direction of Dr. Ahmed Kissebah, reckon that the way body fat is distributed can be an indication of how prone one might be to become diabetic. Dr. Kissebah studied a group of women and found that they could roughly be divided into two groups: those who were "top-heavy," with most fat distributed above the waist; and those who carry most of the excess in the hips and thighs. After a number of tests, it transpired that the top-heavy group was more likely to have undiagnosed diabetes than the other group. Why this should be is not yet clear, and Dr. Kissebah is not saying that every deep-bosomed, full-shouldered female is walking around with a faulty insulin factory in her pancreas. But there does seem at least to be a connection, however slight, not only with the amount of body fat but also with where it lies.

However, diabetes never ceases to surprise the medical men. Having learned that diabetes is more common among people who tend to put on weight very readily than among thin people, I, like you no doubt, would tend to think that people eating a lot of sugar and/or fats would tend to succumb to at least mild diabetes more readily than those who do not share these eating habits. That certainly was the assumption of a leading expert in diabetes, Professor Harry Keen of Guy's Hospital in London, who did a survey to try to detect mild cases of diabetes among ordinary people and relate this to their diet. Surprisingly, Dr. Keen found that sugar and fat intake—and remember we're talking here only about mild, undiagnosed diabetes—was not related to the disease. In fact, quite the opposite. People who ate most, including sugar and fats, seemed less likely to have diabetes. This may seem a contradiction of what I've been saying, but on closer inspection Dr. Keen made a discovery that clears up the mystery. He found that people who tend to put on weight easily tend also to eat the least. Among normal people, thin people eat more than the fat ones. The reason is that thin people, according to Dr. Keen, tend to be "energy wasters": they burn up energy far more quickly than other well-padded counterparts. The fat individuals, on the other hand, conserve their energy longer, often storing it as fat, so they need less food. The key, then, to the difference between the two groups is what has been called their "energy throughput." The "energy conservers" pay for their frugality by a tendency toward diabetes, while the spendthrift "energy wasters" are to some degree protected from the disease.

So there are really two lessons to be learned from this research. First, as everyone connected with diabetes knows, too much fat is dangerous. It raises blood sugar levels and generally puts a strain on the bodily systems. But, second, it is no use simply thinking, "I'll eat less to keep slim." The problem is: how much less. If you're one of the energy wasters, you can be fairly self-indulgent before you begin to see the fat beginning to accumulate. If, on the other hand, you are an ill-fated conserver, you may have to be really ruthless with your diet to keep your weight down, and this may mean switching to a high-fiber diet with lots of whole wheat bread, brown rice, pulses, legumes, cereals, and beans, or simply training your digestive system (and your appetite) to accept less of what you are already eating.

In other words—and here is rule four—do not measure the success of your weight-control diet by the number of calories per day you are consuming. The proof of the pudding is in its effects on the eater. One person's "low" calorie intake is another person's unacceptably high over-indulgence.

Enough of the "Thou shalt nots." What about your weight control diet in practice? What *can* you safely eat? Again let me refer you to the tables in the Appendix, where you'll find a guide to the calorie levels of a wide range of foods. You must, in consultation with your doctor or a dietician, decide on a daily calorie target, say as low as 1,000 if you need to lose weight and around 1,500–1,800 for maintaining yourself at a stable level.

Then, having fixed on a target, which you may need to vary if you find it is too high or too low, you should set out to plan your eating day. Unlike carbohydrates, calories are found in virtually all foods. You don't have the advantage of being able to select "free" foods as you can with CHO. Beware, too, of "diabetic products," specially designed to help you. Some are all right, such as low-calorie drinks and salad dressings, but the rest all contain calories. Sorbitol or fructose may not be as dangerous as the sugar they are intended to replace, but they still contain the same level of calories. Saccharin or aspartame (marketed under the brand names of Equal and Nutrasweet) can be used to sweeten tea or coffee, but, as there are known or believed to be risks involved in taking these substances, never exceed more than two tablets or packets a day. Do without if you can. Perhaps the most powerful argument against dietetic foods is not so much their calorie content as their cost. They are usually expensive, often grossly overpriced, and personally I'd rather use the money in other ways.

When you come to planning meals, it will spread the calorie load better if you set a limit for each meal, perhaps 250 if you are on a 1,200-calorie diet, 400 calories if you are on a 2,000-calorie diet. You should broil, roast, braise, or boil food rather than fry it. A constant problem for many diabetics is that carbohydrate and calorie counts for a given foodstuff just don't match. Take one of my favorite cheeses. It's carbohydrate-free but very high in calories (about 120 per ounce). I've always been hooked on cheese, and when I became a diabetic, cheese was an easy grabber. It was like a snack, but you didn't have to cook it like, say, a hamburger. Cheese is so easy, and if you like it you can just take a hunk of Cheddar and it's great. Eating a lot of cheese, I started to put weight on, so I simply had to go easy on it. So here, then, is a typical day's food for me, all told somewhere in the region of 1,000–1,200 calories.

For breakfast I have two thin slices of unbuttered toast and one fried egg or two strips of bacon. After that I have the juice of two oranges. All told, that comes to 40 grams of carbohydrates.

Two hours later I have two crackers (or if I am in America, a bran muffin; they are delicious where I come from) and a cup of lemon tea, which add up to another 10 grams. Then at noon I take another 50 in the form of stewed fruit—prunes and apricots with yogurt, or fresh fruit with cottage cheese followed by, sometimes not always, a piece of cheese with my coffee.

Midafternoon, I have two cookies and a cup of tea, which adds up to another 10. Then at dinnertime I have some kind of meat and vegetable or salad with a small portion of potatoes, and for dessert I have stewed prunes and apricots or fresh fruit salad with cream. This gives me another 30.

Then finally after dinner I'm allowed 20 carbohydrates before I go to bed, and I usually take those in Bournvita and skim milk, because that relaxes me and makes me sleep well. Or, if I'm very hungry, maybe two shredded wheat with skim milk and Sweet 'n Low.

Variations on this theme are as many as your imagination can muster. I like fried eggs for breakfast, though boiled or poached will do just as well and contain fewer calories. Sometimes lunch is a small helping of meat (2 ounces) or fish (say 4 ounces), together with some green vegetables or salad, plus a little potato. As for alcohol, I nowadays drink only wine, perhaps just a glass or two (smallish ones at that) in the evening. I never take alcohol on an empty stomach because it's well known that it lowers blood sugar.

In many respects, what you eat is somehow less important than your attitude toward food. From being a thoughtless, undisciplined eater I have, by virtue of being diabetic, come to introduce a bit of order into what was hitherto chaotic and, frankly, I like it. I like being involved in myself by making sure I know what I am eating and measuring its effects on me. At the same time, with a stubbornness that even my best friends will tell me about, I positively refuse to let diets and calories and carbohydrates run my life as a puppeteer manipulates his dolls. It's me who likes to keep the world on a string, not vice versa.

Discipline apart, "controlled eating," if I can call it that without making it sound too mechanical, has, I think, made me appreciate food more, enjoy flavor and texture a little more fully, learn to put together combinations that I might never have tried before. But remember that the diabetic regime is three-sided. We've dealt with injections and diet. The third man in the story is the main character in the next chapter: exercise.

9

Move It!

There is exercise and there is EXERCISE. The housewives or shopkeepers who keep on the move most of the working day, walking, lifting, cleaning, and so on, are exerting their bodies at one level, while the professional wrestler or the coal miner is doing so at quite another. But, whichever category you come into by virtue of your job— gentle, moderate, or violent exerciser—of one thing I'm certain. We all need exercise of some description to remain healthy. In his recent book on aging, *Getting On* (Granada, 1982), Peter Evans sums it up admirably thus:

> Look around the animal kingdom and you will observe that more or less constant physical activity is, during waking hours, the way creatures great and small stay alive: hunting, avoiding being hunted; sometimes just keeping fit and alert. Humans too, with more than 600 muscles in their bodies to be kept in good working order, need to move around to maintain their physical condition. Indeed, unlike a machine, the parts of which simply wear out with continuing use, the body deteriorates *without* exercise more rapidly than it would otherwise.

And there we might leave the matter altogether, except for the particular needs and restrictions imposed on those of us whose bodies are unable to handle their sugar intake properly. Exercise for the diabetic is both necessary and problematical.

Why I say this is, when you think about it, fairly obvious. To exert the body is to consume some of its energy, so exercise has an effect similar to that of insulin. Indeed, exercise is just as important as a form of diabetes therapy as drug taking and a controlled diet. It helps keep us slim, feeling fresh and alert, and does something to maintain a proper blood sugar balance. All of which is fine, except that the exercise you take, like the dose of insulin you inject, must be appropriate to your needs. From being someone who is potentially hyperglycemic you can, if you exert yourself too vigorously at the wrong time of day, find yourself in the teeth of a full-scale hypoglycemic attack: sweating, feeling weak, trembling, and confused. So it's vital to remember—and I say this from experience—that your healthy way of life is a juggling act. You're manipulating three clubs—insulin (or pills), exercise, *and* diet—and unless you have all three going nicely in a coordinated fashion, the whole act can collapse in a heap.

So, because physical activity mimics the action of insulin, always remember to compensate for abnormal levels of exercise by taking on board some extra sugar: let the peppermint-ball saga be your constant reminder of this. But how much is "extra"? Well, it varies, of course, with the kind of activity you're engaged in. If I'm rehearsing, say, a fairly hectic scene with lots of comings and goings or gnashings and wailings, I reckon I'm going to need one or two extra 10 g/CHO portions *before* getting into the action. No doubt a diabetic oarsman or rodeo rider takes a 20–50 g/CHO precautionary top-up before performing. Only by judgment and experience (for good or ill) will you arrive at the supplement necessary for *you*. As a general rule, though, take it *before* you exercise. And try to ensure that you exercise after a meal, when your blood sugar level is at a peak, rather than before, when it is in a trough. That way you should avoid the extremes of a hyper or hypo. And another thing, don't ever go out and about, especially if you're doing something strenuous, without a measured CHO supplement in your pocket. A chocolate bar or a glucose tablet, I find, is both easy to carry and easy to use as a regulator.

As to which form of exercise you take, the choice is really determined both by your own preference and by your age group. For me, it's walking. Every day. I walk to almost every place I go to work or to play.

Walking is so good for you. It clears your head and makes you want to work. In America I once worked with Janet Blair, an extremely talented actress. She played the title role in the musical *Mame*. I did Vera to her Mame and we toured the States. I have played Mame myself since, and it is a very taxing role. Janet would sleep all day and then get out of bed and do the show that night, but she didn't really get with it until the second act. She used to complain that her throat bothered her. Well, ask any dancer, you can't walk onto the Covent Garden stage without having warmed up, and my warming up as an actress is walking and talking: to the cab driver; to the waiter; talking to people all day long, getting my mind up and going and fresh, and by the time I get on stage I'm all exercised and everything's loose.

The wonderful thing about diabetes is that, nine times out of ten, when you are taking care of the diabetes you are taking care of other parts of your body, because the diet and the upkeep usually help every other organ in your body as well, which is good, healthy, clean living. Exercise is good for anybody. It happens to agree with the diabetic in particular.

When I first went into the London Clinic they gave me some set exercises to do which, being a receptive, almost childlike patient, I dutifully worked through every day. But frankly I found—and still find—that kind of one-two-three-change exercise extremely boring. I'd much rather be changing the scenery around me by being out there on the move, preferably in the country but just as effectively in the center of town.

Walking may not be *your* thing. So here are a few guidelines to help you decide what is an appropriate alternative for you.

Younger Age Groups

Team and individual games, including strenuous athletics, should be played. Running, jogging, jumping, swimming, football, baseball, soccer, ice or field hockey, tennis, golf, squash, volleyball, basketball, boxing, wrestling, lacrosse, racquetball, rowing, cycling, and so on are all appropriate, provided you take a precautionary carbohydrate portion or portions beforehand. Winter sports such as skiing and skating are acceptable too, as long as extremities are protected.

Middle-aged People

Again, regular exercise but of a less violent nature will suit the majority—activities such as fishing, bowling, gardening, and bird watching. Faster, harder games are not altogether ruled out, though, if you've always been reasonably active. Swimming is ideal, but so, too, are jogging, tennis, sailing, cycling, and water sports. Remember to work up to peak activity levels slowly. At the first sign of strain, rest up and take it easy.

The Elderly

Obviously, do not try to do too much, but do whatever you do regularly and for enjoyment as well as health. Once more I can do no better than refer you here to Peter Evans's excellent book *Getting On*, which devotes considerable space to exercises specially designed for those of you who may be restricted in your recreational opportunities. If you're reasonably fit, of course, there's little you cannot do that's listed above for the middle-aged. If, on the other hand, you are unfortunate enough to have, say, joint problems as well as diabetes, don't despair. There are exercises aplenty for you, too.

One further word on exercise, aimed specifically at female diabetics. Do not let the fact that every month you are all too obviously the target for hormonal changes during menstruation limit your exercise ambitions. Periods are not, whatever you may have been told, incompatible with physical activity, unless of course they make you miserably ill. Then forget it. I don't believe in hair shirts. Be good to yourself, within limits.

And finally, if you are addicted to a sport and will not be deterred from pursuing it, you will no doubt have worked out your own strategies for coping with the need to eat regularly to keep your body balanced. Long-distance swimmers, for example, find that they can best carry their carbohydrates in the form of sugar lumps, sealed by a rubber band in a plastic bag, to tide them over. With a little forethought you, too, will be able to devise gadgets and containers to keep your CHO within reach, whether you are jogging cross-country or sailing along the coast. Diabetics can do most sports, often to a high level of performance. They are not debarred from winning competitions and carrying off the medals. But for the vast majority of us, more important than winning prizes is the twin benefit of feeling in good physical shape and knowing that one is thereby helping to cope with an ever-present disease. Diabetes is not an illness for those who enjoy being an "invalid." That word "invalid" I reckon should be avoided at all costs. If ever I knew a disease in which you were not only able to look after yourself but look after yourself more thoroughly than most people, it's diabetes. It just takes a little determination. So take it from me: as far as exercise is concerned, keep moving.

10

Where Are You Taking Us?

Right from the first moment I was told that I had diabetes, as I said earlier, it was also impressed upon me that there was quite a lot to learn about the condition if I was to come to terms with it. Did I say "quite a lot"? That really was the understatement of all time, because I have not stopped picking up new pieces of information and insight as I go along. Much of this has filtered through from conversations with my doctor or fellow diabetics, sometimes from a magazine article. But there is one aspect of diabetes that has so fascinated me that I've gone out of my way to find out more about it: the dogged fight by medical researchers to understand diabetes fully and perhaps to crack it once and for all.

Perhaps as an actress I'm impressed by the dramatic side of things: the way, for example, Banting and Best transformed the lives and expectations of millions of diabetics virtually overnight when they gave the world insulin; the way a condition of "too much blood sugar" has profound repercussions on everything one is and does—and, of course, presents one with a challenge equal to any part on any stage I can think of; and more.

So I began, a couple of years ago, to do a little of my own research into diabetes, by monitoring the state of play in the laboratories—and there are many of them around the world—where the diabetes jigsaw is being carefully pieced together. The picture is far from complete, but the outlines are unmistakable.

In the course of my browsing I came across some curious little snippets. There was the California doctor who suddenly began to take an interest in people who incessantly scratched their heads, even though their hair had been scrupulously washed and even treated with medication. In several such cases, the scratchers also turned out to have diabetes, and their torments disappeared when their condition was controlled. So, reasoned the good doctor, if you rule out scalp infection or emotional problems, persistent head scratching could be a warning sign of "itchy diabetes." Another odd phenomenon came to light when a team of U.S. doctors at the Marshall University School of Medicine treated a fifty-six-year-old diabetic who had got out of control, having stopped taking his insulin. He was immediately put back on the hormone, together with a low-calorie diet, but still his blood glucose roamed high in the 300–400 mg per milliliter range. There was nothing wrong with his eating habits except that he regularly chewed tobacco. On closer inspection this was found to be "candified" and the patient was swallowing the glucose-rich juice, thereby keeping his blood sugar in a dangerously high state.

Within the mainstream of diabetes research the problems facing the medical scientist are considerable. These have to do with producing more and better insulin, delivering it at the best times, perhaps dispensing with it altogether, and, of course, trying to prevent people's needing it in the first place.

Let's look first at insulin research as such. Wonderful though injections have proved to be, for me and everyone else with a defective pancreas, doctors have long realized that the preparations available are not ideal. For one thing, as I mentioned in Chapter 6, there are cases where people have a reaction to insulin from one kind of animal and have to switch to another type. A second limitation is that diabetic control using an animal hormone is not, of course, as finely tuned as it would be if the source of the insulin were human tissue. Unfortunately, there is not a large supply of human pancreases available to provide the preferable alternative.

Researchers therefore have set to work to find a substitute for animal insulin that gives the benefits of the human substance without undesirable side effects. Their efforts have taken them into some exciting areas of drug development. Perhaps the most intriguing results are coming from those laboratories experimenting with the novel and powerful methods of genetic engineering. Here the scientists have stopped relying on pigs and cows but started instead to do business with a microscopically small bacterium. What happens is this: the genetic blueprint for human insulin is wrapped up in the molecule known as DNA—that complex double-helix-shaped assemblage of atoms which, when described by Francis Crick, James Watson, and Maurice Wilkins, won them a Nobel Prize.

This insulin-producing gene is really a set of coded instructions which, in normal individuals, provide the pancreas with the information to make the hormone. Now, human insulin could be made outside a human pancreas, in some other animal tissue, provided the creature was acting on the correct DNA instructions. What genetic engineers have done is use as the host the bacterium *Escherichia coli*. The human DNA is cleverly inserted into the bacterium, which then, as is its wont, begins to multiply ferociously, at the same time manufacturing insulin: a living, growing drug factory. *Humulin*, as this insulin made by bacteria from human DNA codes is called, is available in the United States and costs about the same amount per vial as purified pork insulin. There are theoretical advantages to the use of this insulin, as it *seems* to result in less antibody production after long-term use. It differs from the "old" conventional beef or pork insulins in terms of onset of action and duration of action, so that your physician may advise changes in dose or timing of injections. Many exciting research studies are under way to see if this new insulin has practical advantages over the old insulins, particularly with regard to incidence of complications of diabetes (long-term).

So far this technique is still in its infancy but, like *E. coli*, it is growing apace. Volunteers have undergone trials with insulin produced in this way with promising results, and big business is taking an interest in biotechnology as a way of boosting its profits. So the future could be rosy for "engineered" insulin in vast quantities.

Another approach to making insulin is to try to synthesize it in the laboratory by purely chemical means. This is not as easy as it sounds, by the way. You don't just decide what chemicals insulin is made of, then make up a mixture from off-the-shelf compounds. It requires intimate knowledge of the molecular structure and properties of insulin, at a depth that so far has not been achieved. But progress is being made in American, British, German, and Scandinavian laboratories, among others.

From time to time medical research gets a lead from some unexpected quarters. This happened a year or two back with diabetes research when it was found that a certain plant, a creeper called *Coccinia indica* which grows in Bengal and which has been part of the Bengali vegetable intake for a long time, seemed to help in diabetes—not the kind that requires insulin but the milder forms. In fact, doctors carried out a trial on a group of such diabetics, putting the plant substance into pills, with promising results. Perhaps this might be yet another weapon in the regular antidiabetes armory of the future?

Taking pills is possible only in mild diabetes. Insulin can't be taken orally because in our digestive juice are enzymes that destroy the hormone before it has a chance to act. However, a British scientist working in Israel, Professor Max Donbrow, has been experimenting with insulin delivered not by injection but by suppository, a method of drug taking that is quite popular in many countries, especially in Europe. So far about five times as much insulin is needed by suppository as by injection to ensure that the hormone gets to work properly, but Professor Donbrow hopes that this can be reduced substantially. To date, his experiments have been only on animals, but if he can overcome this problem of quantity *and* get results in humans, diabetics could enter the age of needleless insulin administration. Experiments are also under way with insulin that can be administered through the nose, like snuff. Good-bye Pincushion City!

Even if suppositories do not prove to be the answer, I reckon that injections may for many people become out of date anyway, thanks to a remarkable little machine being developed in Britain at the National Institute for Medical Research, with clinical tests being carried out at Guy's Hospital under Professor Harry Keen. In fact, already a number of British diabetics who, like me, are insulin-dependent, have used this machine—the portable, miniature insulin infuser—with considerable success. It is the size of a book, worn strapped to the hip, linked by a fine tube to a little needle slipped under the skin. In it is a supply of insulin. Now, the problem with insulin injections, be they one or two shots a day, is that they produce peaks and troughs of drug levels and blood sugar levels. So they do not mimic the normally functioning pancreas, which produces, twenty-four hours a day, exactly the right amount of the hormone needed by the body. The insulin infuser or pump is designed to do just that. It monitors blood sugar levels constantly—and delivers enough insulin to maintain balance. There is none of the under- or over-dosing inevitable with conventional drug delivery systems. This type of pump is called a *closed-loop pump*, as it not only delivers the insulin but also senses the glucose in the blood.

This pump not only has the advantage of tailoring the drug to the condition. By keeping the metabolism of the diabetic on an even keel permanently, doctors hope that they will be able to avoid the long-term effects of diabetes, such as the damage to the eyes that even many controlled diabetics suffer nowadays. This really is an exciting prospect all around, so I am glad to say that laboratories outside Britain are also working on the pump idea. Smaller and less expensive than the closed-loop pump is the *open-loop pump*. Thousands are currently in use in the United States. This pump has no sensor for blood glucose but rather just delivers insulin at a constant "basal" rate and in "boluses" before meals or snacks. The wearer programs the amount of insulin for the basal infusion and for each pre-meal bolus, adjusting the infusion according to the results of blood sugars checked via home glucose monitoring (which was discussed in Chapter 5).

In many respects the pump can be thought of as a major step toward the goal that researchers have been eyeing for many years: the artificial, implantable pancreas. As yet we're still in the realms of theory rather than practicalities, but again the signs are nothing if not hopeful. At a recent medical equipment fair, French scientists showed a prototype microprocessor-controlled artificial pancreas, which monitors the level of sugars in the diabetic patient's blood, compares this figure with its built-in memory of what the level ought to be, and corrects it by administering more or less insulin.

Clearly more research is going to be needed before this device replaces insulin injections or infusing, particularly research into solving the problem of rejection by the body into which the artificial organ is being transplanted. Here I ought to mention some work done at the Harvard Medical School by Dr. William Chick, who has proved that an artificial pancreas—a composite of glass, plastic, and living beta (or insulin-producing) cells—can work for a while in diabetic animals, in this case rats. Chick's machine is remarkable because it combines living cells with the inanimate housing in which they are kept alive, and the whole package was not rejected by the host rats. Maybe this kind of hybrid pancreas will be the sort of device that will be implanted successfully in humans? Incidentally, Russian doctors using an artificial pancreas that's topped up with insulin every few months by injection claim to have been successful with a transplant in a human subject. So progress is undoubtedly being made.

When we talk of transplants, we normally think of kidney or cornea grafts, where the recipient's body gets the healthy organ of a human donor. What are the chances of pancreas transplants, say, from someone who recently died in an accident and whose tissue is compatible with that of a diabetic? Could pancreases be taken from dead donors, frozen, and then transplanted later on? Well, pancreas transplant surgery, though it has proved to be immensely difficult, has met with some success, and I'd like to predict that it will be of benefit to quite a few diabetics before the 1980s are out. A British doctor, Paul McMasters, gave a woman patient both a new kidney and a new pancreas in tandem with her own pancreas, and she did very well on them, being no longer diabetic. More operations followed with a handful of patients as fully recovered as that first lady. Two more actually died during surgery and another two rejected their grafts but carried on with their old, defective pancreases. So there is room for optimism, albeit qualified. Other doctors have tried transplanting not the whole pancreas but either the islet cells that make the insulin or about a third of the whole organ. These experiments have been with animals so far, and unfortunately the results have not been very encouraging.

Prevention, of course, is better than cure, however effective that might be. So some researchers are looking to see what can be done in that direction. When a ten-year-old American boy died suddenly after contracting a particularly savage form of diabetes, doctors found proof of something they'd suspected for years, that in some cases a virus is involved. In fact, they isolated the virus concerned from the dead boy's pancreatic cells—and it has been found in other diabetics, too. The hope here is that they might either be able to develop a vaccine or at least mitigate the more drastic effects of the virus. Another important line of work came out of the chance observation that more than half the people who suffer from adult-onset diabetes often get embarrassing red facial flushes when they drink alcohol. Some very clever research has shown that this is linked with levels of the substance enkephalin, which is manufactured in the brain. It appears that enkephalin is concerned with the *control* of the liberation of insulin from the pancreas and that in these mature-onset diabetics the fault lies not in the pancreas itself but in the control center in the brain. This discovery opens up new avenues of diabetes control, and a lot of hard work to this end is presently being carried out in laboratories both in the United Kingdom and the United States.

Elsewhere clues to the causes of diabetes are being sought by nutritionists. One such scientist, Dr. Walter Mertz of the U.S. Department of Agriculture, believes that some diabetics may owe their disease to a vitamin deficiency—namely, a lack of chromium in the diet—

which makes them unable to use insulin efficiently. So he is looking into this further. Other doctors are concentrating on preventing not so much the disease itself as some of its complications. Dr. Kenneth Gabby at Harvard University reckons that some of the diabetics' associated symptoms, such as damage to the arterial system, the nerves, and the eyes, might be helped by blocking off the supply of excess glucose to these parts of the body, using a special chemical blocker. His experiments on diabetic rats showed that the chemical did to some extent prevent cataracts in the eyes of one group while the others, fed an equal amount of excess sugar, fared relatively badly. A glimmer of hope for sufferers of painful diabetic neuropathy comes from two laboratories that used a new drug, sorbilil, to improve muscle strength and sensation in patients with severe neuropathy unresponsive to other medications. More studies are in progress. Once more we will have to wait and see.

And, finally, here's a thought to conjure with: the case of the inadequate mouse milk, as related by broadcaster Alan Stennett:

> A research team at the Diabetics Institute at Düsseldorf University ran into a problem when it found it couldn't get enough mouse milk, the raw material for its work. The problem wasn't a shortage of mice, it was a shortage of milkers—it's not just a matter of small hands and a very low stool. The difficulty was sorted out by ordering a miniature milking machine from a specialist firm in the United States, and having it flown over to Germany, although the airline concerned did admit to being rather suspicious when first approached. They thought it was all a hoax (to quote one of the airline officials, "we thought someone was taking the Mickey"). The machine has now been installed in a "mouse milking parlour" at the university, and the researchers are assured of an ample supply of

milk. Exactly how much milk a mouse gives is not known, and the mouse machine is not fitted with the recording devices usual to conventional milking machines. One researcher was asked to make an estimate but his reply was: "Not very much," so it may be that quite a lot of mice will be needed to help the workers towards their aim of a cure for the many human sufferers from diabetes.

(*Source:* BBC External Services/Central Talks and Features: "Of Mice and Men and Milking Machines?")

11
Has It Changed My Life?

Of course it has. But in unexpected ways. And on balance—no pun intended—for the better. I must confess I was extremely apprehensive at first about the whole idea of being permanently "ill" and what it might do to my career, and from time to time I worry that the real problem lies in other people, in the stigma that attaches to anyone who is different. I have a feeling that some producers who have got $500,000 on the boards will say, "Well, now hold it, hold it, wait a minute, she's got diabetes." I will fight this to my dying day because a controlled, intelligent, humorous, up-to-snuff diabetic is in better shape than any actor in the world.

Once a real dumb actor (and a dumb actor is a bad actor—and he, poor darling, was dumb and bad) came up to me and said, "Listen, can I give you a little bit of advice?" and I said, "Sure."

He said, "I think you're nuts."

Elaine: "Thank you very much. What else is new?"

He said, "You've just come out of the hospital with diabetes and you're giving interviews about it. Cool it."

I said, "Why?"

Now, this must have been a person who had really been through the mill as an actor because he said, "You'll never work again."

103

I thought to myself, oh my God, what an idiot! and said, "If I never worked again it would only mean that all the directors and producers in showbiz are as dopey as you are!"

I would rather never set my foot on the stage again than keep quiet about the fact that I'm a diabetic or anything else for that matter. My life, I'm afraid, is an open book, and I, along with most of the people I know, like it that way.

I've never used having diabetes to get away with things, but I've joked about it. The first thing I said to Hal Prince when I got it was "You'll never get me to stay ten minutes beyond the lunch break now." And everybody laughed.

Now, Hal may go home and say, "Oh, there's another problem." But your being honest should make it easier, depending on the people around you. Once a producer grumbled to me, "I don't know, we have these problems with you; we used to blame the drinking, now we don't know what to blame."

"Try the director," I said.

If the situation presents itself where they have to know I've got it, I'm going to be totally open about it, because there's nothing to be ashamed of. If they hijack your plane and you've got diabetes, tell the hijackers and ask them if they can get a little insulin on board. Be honest. Who knows, you may be the first one off the plane.

It's funny, but I think diabetes in a strange way was for me a godsend. The crazy fears that I've had all my life about performing, about being accepted in society, accepted socially, accepted by men, by women, had worn my nervous system to a frazzle. Maybe that was a contributing factor—could be.

With diabetes I have a legitimate reason for taking care of myself, and I do so fearlessly. My inclination in the past was to go until I dropped. I'd rehearse until four in the morning, I didn't care what the other members of the company did. I would work on whatever I was involved in until I dropped, extending myself too far for my own good. In the past I could never say, "I'm sorry but I have to have my dinner now—I can't work through the dinner hour, I have to eat, I'm hungry, I'm tired, I'm miserable . . ." because I was afraid to admit it, and I would wear down my nervous system, then suffer as a result. Now I can very legitimately say, "I've had enough. It's time to take a break." It's almost like an imaginary Mommy and Big Daddy backing me up—diabetes, that is—so now after five hours of strenuous rehearsals I simply say, "That's it, folks, for a while, unless you dig hypos."

What aggravates me is when somebody complains that people who are unaware of my diabetes get upset if I have to have something to eat on the set after my insulin shot. I say to my producer, "Then make them aware of it, please! Thank you very much."

You can't say that because you've got a disease you've had your share of hardships, and no others are going to come your way. I could say I've got diabetes, so that's enough already. Well, it sometimes isn't enough. Sometimes other hardships come your way, and that's when it's tough with diabetes. I've always been pretty good with the big problems that life presents. Catastrophes I can handle very well. The house could be on fire and I keep my cool. Everybody follow me and I'll get us out of this or any other situation that's a big deal, but—and it's a big "but"—if I can't find my glasses I go out of my mind. I have to watch this because nowadays I have not only this compelling desire for routine but also a little paranoia in the "place for everything, everything in its place" department. This has its dangers, because you have to be careful you don't turn into an organization addict: "I can't move now, it's time for my cookies," and my husband would say, "Why don't you have a banana instead of those?"

I'd say, "Because I have two cookies. I'm used to two cookies. I want the two cookies. Bananas have no part in my life!" Spoilt brat. Right? Right!

Well, what the hell! I feel that there are only a few treats in the day for me and I want them the way I want them.

However, diabetes has provided my life with a measure of organization and discipline that was sorely lacking before. But I don't want to get to the stage where my mind and body are permanently on automatic pilot, where I never do anything at all that is not preplanned, prepacked, and preexperienced. Life must retain a measure of the unexpected and unpredictable, otherwise it's robot time in Dixie.

As an actress I've "used" diabetes—not to cop out of responsibility, that's not my style, but just for a laugh I might say to a director, "Don't raise your voice to me, I'm a diabetic!" But seriously, my big thing is to excel in energy, to make myself better than the person who doesn't have diabetes.

The way I've really exploited my condition is to squeeze every bit of dramatics out of it that I can. When leaving the cocktail party to take my shot I might say, "It's time for my fix" or "I'm about to shoot up, I'll be right back." Why not call attention to the fact that you're different and get a few laughs into the bargain?

If the good Lord sends you diabetes, why not make a movie out of it. Who knows? You might win an "emotional Oscar" . . . the best kind.

One of the biggest changes that diabetes has produced in me is an awareness of other people's problems, especially other diabetics'. I've just been talking about "being different," but things *are* different when the diabetic happens to be a youngster. I've come across a number of young diabetics and their parents when I've been speaking at, say, a luncheon organized by the British Diabetic Association or opening a fete or something. And whenever I speak to children who are diabetic I'm constantly reminded that kids *don't want* to be different. So perhaps you have to approach the condition in children from a different point of view. With the kids it isn't a matter of standing out in a crowd. They're not after that. Most kids like to look like the rest of the gang. What kids get satisfaction from is the fact that they have the responsibility for handling their own life. Some children, when they accomplish something that's difficult and very adult-like, get satisfaction out of it whether they let their friends know or not. But I think the best way to approach kids with diabetes is straight on. They like it that way. Explain the cause. Explain the reason and get on with it. Save the Beatrix Potter drawings for the adults. Like me. For instance, my favorite book on diabetes is one that uses a popular character from British children's books—"Rupert the Bear." A bear with diabetes. That's my style. When I read that book I got more information than I ever did from grown-up books. Get the message? Treat the little kids like the big kids, and vice versa.

I'm a fairly well known actress and very open about my diabetes. As a result, the meetings I have had personally with diabetics, not to mention the conversations I've had on the phone with diabetics, are unbelievable. Sometimes sad, sometimes funny, but always rewarding, and I might add time-consuming, but oh so well spent. A woman called me the other day and said, "I've thought about calling you for the last six months and finally got the nerve." (It just breaks your heart when you think of people going through that.) She said, "My sister is diabetic and has been on the pills and now they tell her she's got to take insulin. But she refuses to take it and they say, well, she's going to die, and she says, 'I'm fifty-two. What do I care?' "

"My God," I said, "what do you mean?"

She's younger than I am. Not much but a little. Now, the diabetic sister apparently is a big fan of mine, and she watches me on television, so her healthy sister thought if a stranger, and a famous actress to boot, took an interest, it might change her mind about leaving the building at fifty-two. So I said, "Look, before we get to your sister, let's do you some good. First of all you don't have to apologize for calling me, it's wonderful that you did."

I then phoned her diabetic sister and said, "Elaine Stritch here. Now listen, Elizabeth, I haven't got time to fool around."

She says, "Oh, my sister's called you."

I said, "Yes, she did. Let's not go through all that and get me in a big family row."

"Oh no, I don't mind that she did it," she says, "but, Miss Stritch, much as I admire you, and I do think you're very talented, I'm not going to take any insulin."

So I said, "The big plan of your sister isn't going to work, then, is that what you're telling me?"

"Well, I don't know about that . . ." she replied.

I said, "Don't waste much time thanking me, then, because I find you very insensitive. I've taken time and am paying for a long-distance call to see if I could knock some sense into you. Do you believe the doctor when he tells you you're going to die if you don't take any insulin?"

"Maybe I do, maybe I don't, but I'm at an age when I'm not putting any of that phony stuff in my body to keep me alive."

And I said, "You idiot, you don't like the idea of putting something inside to keep you alive? What do you think people are doing when they're eating every day? People who need vitamins take vitamins every day."

"I know," she says, "but I was getting along fine on the pills."

I said, "Apparently your pancreas is not doing anything for you now and how do you think those two guys Banting and Best would feel if *they* heard this nonsense from you? After all they went through to keep all of us diabetics alive."

"Well, I know you mean well," says she.

I could have killed her. I said, "I'll tell you what to do, just die, Elizabeth. Maybe you have a death wish. Ever think about that? Your doctor's not nuts, you know. I mean, that would be the most wonderful way in the world for me to commit suicide—I'd get very thin and I'd go out a few times in a very good-looking dress, because I love being thin, Elizabeth, so I'd just go through that and get down to about 90 pounds and then I'd die if I didn't take my insulin. What do you think's making me take my insulin, and you say you won't take it?"

"Well, I . . . I . . . I just . . ." She stuttered and stammered around for a while and I got really mad and was determined to shake her up a lot. I won't repeat my language on the phone (after all, I want kids to be allowed to read this book), but the story has a happy ending. Elizabeth is now religiously injecting two shots a day. Praise the Lord and pass the medi-swabs!

More often I get letters, lots of them, asking: "How do you manage? What do you do? Do you get depressed? Are you frightened? Do you get this or that?" and so on. And I usually write a short letter and see that I take every opportunity I get to do an interview or put in print what I believe. It sure pays off in my mind and heart and, who knows, maybe saves a life or two. . . .

I constantly find that I have to remind healthy people of what diabetes is all about, or rather what it *isn't* all about. They tend to think that the diabetic regime is totally removed from their own freewheeling life-style. One day an actor, Ralph something or other, came up to me at rehearsal and said, as I was putting my prunes and apricots into a bowl with yogurt for the lunch break, "Do you have that *every* day for lunch?" with this terrible expression on his face.

I felt like saying, "Thanks a lot, have you got any more good news for me?" But all I replied was "Yes I do." I left it for half an hour, because I was so mad at him I thought I was going to kill him—bad enough to have diabetes without someone leaning over your shoulder and being sniffy about what you eat. Then I went across the room to him and said, "Let me ask you something, Ralph. What do you have for breakfast in the morning?"

He said, "I have a fried egg and a couple of pieces of bacon and four slices of whole wheat."

He slowed down and I asked, "Do you have that every morning?"

And he said, "To hell with you, Elaine." Every morning he had exactly the same thing, regular as clockwork, but I'm the one, poor thing, who's stuck on the same dish every day. Anyway I like, actually like, prunes, apricots, and yogurt. So there, Ralph!

12
Reflections, and Au Revoir

How I wish I could wake up on a sunny morning and take a walk with nothing in my hands. Diabetes is excess baggage. In spades. I'm used to it now, but I still have that dream of being prop-free. I don't want lunch today, let's go to the moon today. No shots today (insulin, that is). Let's have chocolate mousse and whipped cream for breakfast today. But, alas, these thoughts are fantasy. So what! I can dream, can't I?

More than the problems of organizing my injections and exercise and food, I find that diabetes has forced me to take stock of people, situations, and events that are likely to trigger off emotional stress, because the more stressed I am, the worse I feel and, more important, the less able I am to cope. This doesn't mean withdrawing from hard work and excitement. Don't diminish your activities in any way, but try to be aware of potentially stressful situations—socially, for instance. "So-and-so asked me to dinner and it'll hurt his/her feelings if I don't go." And so on. Well, if you can get yourself in a frame of mind to know exactly what you're doing—and as I've said before, you can rehearse at home how you're going to be at dinner and make a game out of it—all may be well. But if you're going to go and spend time with people who make you nervous, then don't go. *You* have to be number one, have no doubts or qualms about that. Be egotistical about yourself, make yourself number one and *keep* yourself number one. It's a hell of a help to your marriage when you're diabetic. As I said earlier, I've never used diabetes as a cop-out or an excuse, but I've got humor out of it and I also noticed that my husband ceased to argue with me about unimportant things, because it wasn't worth it. He didn't want to see me upset. It was as simple as that.

My attitude to my life as a diabetic is simply this: I want to be the *best* diabetic in the whole world. And believe me, humor has a great deal to do with the success of this ambition.

To become the ideal diabetic, I prescribe a lot of laughter. Humor—what a loaded noun! I don't mean wearing a lampshade at parties, I mean seeing the humorous side of something that's difficult for you; people who've had difficult things to cope with in life will agree that a sense of humor not only helps, it *saves* your life! If I find that I have adapted to a disciplined life, and acquired a respect for moderation in the last five years, then diabetes can't be all bad. Moderation, incidentally, is more exciting and satisfying to anyone who has been excessive in the past. I think even Orson Welles would feel better at the end of the day if he had had three sirloin steaks for lunch instead of six. Well, Orson, it is a step in the right direction. . . .

I'll never forget the round, very, very well endowed black lady who worked in the ladies' room of a Mayfair night spot. I had retired discreetly, as they say, in order to give myself an injection and was poised, syringe in hand, ready to take the shot when in walked the said lady. The look of incredulity mingled with outrage on her face had to be seen to be believed.

She cried out, "Hell, now look what's going on around here," and ran away upstairs, saying she was going to quit. She says, "I ain't gonna work noplace where they're shooting up in the ladies'," and I had to go up to her and explain all about diabetes and she left me with a kind of uh-huh sort of "I'll bet." You just can't win them all. But at the end of the day, the pluses of diabetes are, I can honestly say, outweighing the minuses. I'm in several important respects healthier than during my prediabetic days. I feel fit, in control, and well adjusted, and it's no exaggeration to say that I owe so much of this to diabetes. I hope this doesn't sound as if I'm somehow glorying in diabetes. In truth I've never much subscribed to the Trouper Myth—that the show must go on, that you must smile through the tears, and there's pleasure in distress, etc. What I'm saying is that diabetes is something I am managing not only to live with, but to enjoy life with more than ever. And if I can do it, so can you. Am I blue?

Yes, if I play my cards right, morning, noon, and night.

Appendix 1
Food Lists

In this appendix are the updated (1976) Exchange Lists for Meal Planning prepared by committees of the American Diabetes Association and the American Dietetic Association in cooperation with the National Institute of Arthritis, Metabolism and Digestive Diseases and the National Heart and Lung Institute, the National Institutes of Health, the Public Health Service, and the U.S. Department of Health, Education and Welfare (now Health and Human Services). The lists are groups of measured foods of approximately the same nutritional and caloric value. The groups are called exchanges because foods in any one group can be substituted or exchanged with other foods in the same group in meal plans. ©American Diabetes Association, Inc., The American Dietetic Association, 1976. All rights reserved under International and Pan-American Copyright Convention.

MILK EXCHANGES

One exchange of milk contains 12 grams of carbohydrate, 8 grams of protein, a trace of fat, and 80 calories. Milk products appearing in bold type are nonfat. Low-fat and whole-milk listings contain saturated fat.

Nonfat Fortified Milk

Skim or nonfat milk	1 cup
Powdered (nonfat dry, before adding liquid)	⅓ cup
Canned, evaporated skim milk	½ cup
Buttermilk made from skim milk	1 cup
Yogurt made from skim milk (plain, unflavored)	1 cup

Low-Fat Fortified Milk

1% fat fortified milk (omit ½ Fat Exchange)	1 cup
2% fat fortified milk (omit 1 Fat Exchange)	1 cup
Yogurt made from 2% fortified milk (plain, unflavored) (omit 1 Fat Exchange)	1 cup

Whole Milk (Omit 2 Fat Exchanges)

Whole milk	1 cup
Canned, evaporated whole milk	½ cup
Buttermilk made from whole milk	1 cup
Yogurt made from whole milk (plain, unflavored)	1 cup

VEGETABLE EXCHANGES

One exchange of vegetables (½ cup) contains about 5 grams of carbohydrate, 2 grams of protein, and 25 calories.

Asparagus
Bean sprouts
Beets
Broccoli
Brussels sprouts
Cabbage
Carrots
Cauliflower
Celery
Eggplant
Green pepper
Greens:
   Beet
   Chards
   Collards
   Dandelion
   Kale

Mustard
Spinach
Turnip
Mushrooms
Okra
Onions
Rhubarb
Rutabaga
Sauerkraut
String beans, green or yellow
Summer squash
Tomatoes
Tomato juice
Turnips
Vegetable juice cocktail
Zucchini

The following raw vegetables may be used as desired:

Chicory
Chinese cabbage
Cucumbers
Endive
Escarole
Lettuce
Parsley
Pickles, dill
Radishes
Watercress

Starchy Vegetables are found in the bread exchange list.

FRUIT EXCHANGES

One exchange of fruit contains 10 grams of carbohydrate and 40 calories. Fruit may be used fresh, dried, canned or frozen, cooked or raw, as long as no sugar is added.

Apple	1 small
Apple juice	⅓ cup
Applesauce (unsweetened)	½ cup
Apricots, dried	4 halves
Apricots, fresh	2 medium
Banana	½ small
Berries	
Blackberries	½ cup
Blueberries	½ cup
Raspberries	½ cup
Strawberries	¾ cup
Cherries	10 large
Cider	⅓ cup
Dates	2
Figs, dried	1
Figs, fresh	1
Grapefruit	½
Grapefruit juice	½ cup
Grapes	12
Grape juice	¼ cup
Mango	½ small
Melon	
Cantaloupe	¼ small
Honeydew	⅛ medium
Watermelon	1 cup
Nectarine	1 small
Orange	1 small
Orange juice	½ cup
Papaya	¾ cup
Peach	1 medium
Pear	1 small
Persimmon, native	1 medium

Pineapple	½ cup
Pineapple juice	⅓ cup
Plums	2 medium
Prunes	2 medium
Prune juice	¼ cup
Raisins	2 tablespoons
Tangerine	1 medium

Cranberries may be used as desired if no sugar is added.

BREAD EXCHANGES

One exchange of bread contains 15 grams of carbohydrate, 2 grams of protein, and 70 calories. Starchy vegetables are included in this list because they contain the same amount of carbohydrate and protein as one slice of bread. Items appearing in bold type are low-fat.

Bread

White (including French and Italian)	1 slice
Whole wheat	1 slice
Rye or pumpernickel	1 slice
Raisin	1 slice
Bagel, small	½
English muffin, small	½
Plain roll, bread	1
Frankfurter roll	½
Hamburger bun	½
Dried bread crumbs	3 tablespoons
Tortilla, 6″ in diameter	1

Cereal

Bran Flakes	½ cup
Other ready-to-eat unsweetened cereal	¾ cup
Puffed cereal (unfrosted)	1 cup
Cereal (cooked)	½ cup
Grits (cooked)	½ cup
Rice or barley (cooked)	½ cup
Pasta (cooked), Spaghetti, noodles, macaroni	½ cup
Popcorn (popped, no fat added, large kernel)	3 cups
Cornmeal (dry)	2 tablespoons
Flour	2½ tablespoons
Wheat germ	¼ cup

Crackers

Arrowroot	3
Graham, 2½ " square	2
Matzoth, 4" × 6"	½
Oyster	20
Pretzels, 3⅛ " long × ⅛ " diameter	25
Rye Wafers, 2" × 3½ "	3
Saltines	6
Soda, 2½ " square	4

Dried Beans, Peas and Lentils

Beans, peas, lentils (dried and cooked)	½ cup
Baked beans, no pork (canned)	¼ cup

Starchy Vegetables

Corn	⅓ cup
Corn on cob	1 small
Lima beans	½ cup
Parsnips	⅔ cup
Peas, green (canned or frozen)	½ cup
Potato, white	1 small
Potato (mashed)	½ cup
Pumpkin	¾ cup
Winter squash, acorn or butternut	½ cup
Yam or sweet potato	¼ cup

Prepared Foods

Biscuit, 2″ diameter	1
(omit 1 Fat Exchange)	
Corn bread, 2″ × 2″ × 1″	1
(omit 1 Fat Exchange)	
Corn muffin, 2″ diameter	1
(omit 1 Fat Exchange)	
Crackers, round butter type	5
(omit 1 Fat Exchange)	
Muffin, plain small	1
(omit 1 Fat Exchange)	
Potatoes, French fried, length 2″ to 3½″	8
(omit 1 Fat Exchange)	
Potato or corn chips	15
(omit 2 Fat Exchanges)	
Pancake, 5″ × ½″	1
(omit 1 Fat Exchange)	
Waffle, 5″ × ½″	1
(omit 1 Fat Exchange)	

MEAT EXCHANGES

Lean Meat

One exchange of lean meat contains 7 grams of protein, 3 grams of fat, and 55 calories. Other protein-rich foods are included in this list.

Beef:	Baby beef (very lean), chipped beef, chuck, flank steak, tenderloin, plate ribs, plate skirt steak, round (bottom, top), all cuts rump, spare ribs, tripe	1 ounce
Lamb:	Leg, rib, sirloin, loin (roast and chops), shank, shoulder	1 ounce
Pork:	Leg (whole rump, center shank), ham, smoked (center slices)	1 ounce
Veal:	Leg, loin, rib, shank, shoulder, cutlets	1 ounce
Poultry:	Meat without skin of chicken, turkey, Cornish hen, guinea hen, pheasant	1 ounce
Fish:	Any fresh or frozen	1 ounce
	Canned salmon, tuna, mackerel, crab and lobster	¼ cup
	Clams, oysters, scallops, shrimp	5 or 1 ounce
	Sardines, drained	3
Cheeses containing less than 5% butterfat		1 ounce
Cottage cheese, dry and 2% butterfat		¼ cup
Dried beans and peas (omit 1 Bread Exchange)		½ cup

Medium-Fat Meat

One exchange of medium-fat meat contains 7 grams of protein, 5 grams of fat, and 75 calories. Other protein-rich foods are included in this list.

Beef:	Ground (15% fat), corned beef (canned), rib eye, round (ground commercial)	1 ounce
Pork:	Loin (all cuts tenderloin), shoulder arm (picnic), shoulder blade, Boston butt, Canadian bacon, boiled ham	1 ounce
Liver, heart, kidney and sweetbreads (these are high in cholesterol)		1 ounce
Cottage cheese, creamed		¼ cup
Cheese:	Mozzarella, ricotta, farmer's cheese, Neufchâtel	1 ounce
	Parmesan	3 tablespoons
Egg (high in cholesterol)		1
Peanut butter (omit 2 additional Fat Exchanges)		2 tablespoons

High-Fat Meat

One exchange of high-fat meat contains 7 grams of protein, 8 grams of fat, and 100 calories. Other protein-rich foods are included on this list.

Beef:	Brisket, corned beef (brisket), ground beef (more than 20% fat), hamburger (commercial), chuck (ground commercial), roasts (rib), steaks (club and rib)	1 ounce
Lamb:	Breast	1 ounce
Pork:	Spare ribs, loin (back ribs), pork (ground), country-style ham, deviled ham	1 ounce
Veal:	Breast	1 ounce
Poultry:	Capon, duck (domestic), goose	1 ounce
Cheese:	Cheddar types	1 ounce
Cold cuts		4½″ × ⅛″ slice
Frankfurter		1 small

FAT EXCHANGES

One exchange of fat contains 5 grams of fat and 45 calories.
Exchanges that appear in bold type contain polyunsaturated
fat.

Margarine, soft, tub or stick*	1 teaspoon
Avocado (4″ in diameter)**	⅛
Oil, corn, cottonseed, safflower, soy, sunflower	1 teaspoon
Oil, olive**	1 teaspoon
Oil, peanut**	1 teaspoon
Olives**	5 small
Almonds**	10 whole
Pecans**	2 large whole
Peanuts**	
Spanish	20 whole
Virginia	10 whole
Walnuts	6 small
Nuts, other**	6 small
Margarine, regular stick	1 teaspoon
Butter	1 teaspoon
Bacon fat	1 teaspoon
Bacon, crisp	1 strip
Cream, light	2 tablespoons
Cream, sour	2 tablespoons
Cream, heavy	1 tablespoon
Cream cheese	1 tablespoon
French dressing***	1 tablespoon
Italian dressing***	1 tablespoon
Lard	1 teaspoon
Mayonnaise***	1 teaspoon
Salad dressing, mayonnaise type***	2 teaspoons
Salt pork	¾ inch cube

*Made with corn, cottonseed, safflower, soy or sunflower
  oil only
**Fat content is primarily monounsaturated
***If made with corn, cottonseed, safflower, soy or sunflower
  oil can be used on fat modified diet

Appendix 2
American Diabetes Association Affiliates

Alabama Affiliate, Inc.
904 Bob Wallace Avenue
Suite 222
Huntsville, AL 35801
(205) 533-5775 or (205) 533-5776

Alaska Affiliate, Inc.
540 L Street
Suite 202
Anchorage, AK 99501
(907) 276-3607

Arizona Affiliate, Inc.
7337 North 19th Avenue
Room 404
Phoenix, AZ 85021
(602) 995-1515

Arkansas Affiliate, Inc.
Suite 229
Tanglewood Shopping Center
7509 Cantrell Road
Little Rock, AR 72207
(501) 666-9481

Northern California
Affiliate, Inc.
2550 9th Street
Suite 114
Berkeley, CA 94710
(415) 644-0920

Southern California
Affiliate, Inc.
3460 Wilshire Blvd.
Suite #900
Los Angeles, CA 90010
(213) 381-3639

Colorado Affiliate, Inc.
2450 South Downing Street
Denver, CO 80210
(303) 778-7556

Connecticut Affiliate, Inc.
17 Oakwood Avenue
West Hartford, CT 06119
(203) 236-1948

Delaware Affiliate, Inc.
2713 Lancaster Avenue
Wilmington, DE 19805
(302) 656-0030

Washington, D.C. Area
Affiliate, Inc.
4405 East-West Highway
Suite 403
Bethesda, MD 20814
(301) 657-8303

Florida Affiliate, Inc.
P. O. Box 19745
Orlando, FL 32814
3101 Maguire Blvd.
Suite 288 (Street Address)
Orlando, FL 32803
(305) 894-6664

Georgia Affiliate, Inc.
1447 Peachtree Street, N.E.
Suite 810
Atlanta, GA 30309
(404) 881-1963

Hawaii Affiliate, Inc.
510 South Beretania Street
Honolulu, HI 96813
(808) 521-5677

Idaho Affiliate, Inc.
1528 Vista
Boise, ID 83705
(208) 342-2774

Downstate Illinois Affiliate, Inc.
965 No. Water Street
Decatur, IL 62523
(217) 422-8228

Northern Illinois Affiliate, Inc.
6 North Michigan Avenue
Suite 1202
Chicago, IL 60602
(312) 346-1805

Indiana Affiliate, Inc.
222 S. Downey Avenue, Suite 320
Indianapolis, IN 46219
(317) 352-9226

Iowa Affiliate, Inc.
1118 First Avenue, N.E.
Cedar Rapids, IA 52402
(319) 366-6884

Kansas Affiliate, Inc.
2312 East Central
Wichita, KS 67214
(316) 265-6671 (800) 362-1355

Kentucky Affiliate, Inc.
P. O. Box 345
Frankfort, KY 40602
(502) 223-2971

Louisiana Affiliate, Inc.
619 Jefferson Highway
Suite 2B
Baton Rouge, LA 70806
(504) 927-7732

Maine Affiliate, Inc.
59 Northport Ave.
Belfast, ME 04915
(207) 622-3987

Maryland Affiliate, Inc.
3701 Old Court Road
Suite 19
Baltimore, MD 21208
(301) 486-5516

Massachusetts Affiliate, Inc.
377 Elliot Street
Newton Upper Falls, MA 02164
(617) 965-2323

Michigan Affiliate, Inc.
The Clausen Bldg. No. Unit
23100 Providence Dr.
Suite 475
Southfield, MI 48075
(313) 552-0480

Minnesota Affiliate, Inc.
3005 Ottawa Ave., South
Minneapolis, MN 55416
(612) 920-6796

Mississippi Affiliate, Inc.
10 Lakeland Circle
Jackson, MS 39216
(601) 981-9511

Greater St. Louis Affiliate, Inc.
1780 South Brentwood Boulevard
St. Louis, MO 63144
(314) 968-3196

Heart of America Affiliate, Inc.
616 East 63rd Street
Kansas City, MO 64110
(816) 361-3361

Missouri Regional Affiliate, Inc.
P.O. Box 11 (Mailing Address)
811 Cherry
Columbia, MO 65201
(314) 443-8611

Montana Affiliate, Inc.
600 Central Plaza, Suite 304
Box 2411
Great Falls, MT 59401
(406) 761-0908

Nebraska Affiliate, Inc.
7377 Pacific, Suite 216A
Omaha, NE 68114
(402) 391-1251

Nevada Affiliate, Inc.
4000 E. Charleston Blvd.
Las Vegas, NV 89104
(702) 459-7099

New Hampshire Affiliate, Inc.
102 North Main Street
(Street Address)
Manchester, NH 03102
P.O. Box 595
Manchester, NH 03105
(603) 627-9579

New Jersey Affiliate, Inc.
312 North Adamsville Road
P.O. Box 6423
Bridgewater, NJ 08807
(201) 725-7878

New Mexico Affiliate, Inc.
525 San Pedro, N.E., Suite 101
Albuquerque, NM 87108
(505) 266-5716

New York Diabetes Affiliate, Inc.
55 W. 39th Street
New York, NY 10018
(212) 944-7899

New York State Affiliate, Inc.
P.O. Box 1037
Hotel Syracuse, Suite 1137
(Street Address)
Syracuse, NY 13202
(315) 472-9111

Akron Area Affiliate, Inc.
225 West Exchange Street
Akron, OH 44302
(216) 762-7487

Cincinnati Affiliate, Inc.
1216 E. McMillan Street
Cincinnati, OH 45206
(513) 221-2111

Dayton Area Affiliate, Inc.
184 Salem Avenue
Dayton, OH 45406
(513) 225-3002

Greater Ohio Affiliate, Inc.
10340 Cliffwood Road
Perrysburg, OH 43551
(419) 874-1880

Oklahoma Affiliate, Inc.
Kelly Professional Building
6565 So. Yale Avenue
Suite 105
Tulsa, OK 74136
(918) 492-3839 or (800) 722-5448

North Carolina Affiliate, Inc.
Station Square
Suite 50
Rocky Mount, NC 27801
(919) 446-1108

North Dakota Affiliate, Inc.
101 North 3rd St., Ste. 502
(Street Address)
Grand Forks, ND 58201
P.O. Box 234
Grand Forks, ND 58206-0234
(701) 746-4427

Oregon Affiliate, Inc.
3607 S.W. Corbett Street
Portland, OR 97201
(503) 228-0849

Greater Philadelphia
Affiliate, Inc.
The Bourse, Suite 570
21 South Fifth Street
Philadelphia, PA 19106
(215) 627-7718

Western Pennsylvania
Affiliate, Inc.
4617 Winthrop Street
Pittsburgh, PA 15213
(412) 682-3392

Mid-Pennsylvania Affiliate, Inc.
430 E. Broad Street
Bethlehem, PA 18018
(215) 867-6660

Rhode Island Affiliate, Inc.
4 Fallon Avenue
Providence, RI 02908
(401) 331-0099

South Carolina Affiliate, Inc.
2838 Devine Street
Columbia, SC 29205
(803) 799-4246

South Dakota Affiliate, Inc.
P.O. Box 659
Sioux Falls, SD 57101
(605) 342-8450

Greater Tennessee Affiliate, Inc.
Room 226-228
Medical Arts Bldg.
1211 21st Avenue So.
Nashville, TN 37212
(615) 320-0493

Mid-South Affiliate, Inc.
80 N. Tillman, Suite 109
Memphis, TN 38111
(901) 452-1155

Texas Affiliate, Inc.
6201 Middle Fiskville Road
Austin, TX 78752
(512) 454-7614

Utah Affiliate, Inc.
Graystone Plaza, No. 4
1174 East 2700 South
Salt Lake City, UT 84106
(801) 486-4989

Vermont Affiliate, Inc.
217 Church Street
Burlington, VT 05401
(802) 862-3882

Virginia Affiliate, Inc.
404 8th Street, N.E.
Charlottesville, VA 22901
(804) 293-4953

Washington Affiliate, Inc.
3201 Fremont Avenue North
Seattle, WA 98103
(206) 632-4576

West Virginia Affiliate, Inc.
Professional Building
1036 Quarrier Street, Room 404
Charleston, WV 25301
(304) 346-6418 or (800) 642-3055

Wisconsin Affiliate, Inc.
6915 W. Fond du Lac Avenue
Milwaukee, WI 53218
(414) 464-9395

Wyoming Affiliate, Inc.
P.O. Box 15589
Cheyenne, WY 82003
(307) 638-3578

For Further Reading

American Diabetes Association. *Guide to Good Living*. New York: American Diabetes Association, 1983.

American Diabetes Association and the American Dietetic Association. *The American Dietetic Association Family Cookbook*. Englewood Cliffs, N.J.: Prentice-Hall, 1980.

American Diabetes Association and the Metropolitan Medical Center. *Diabetes: Recipes for Health*. Bowie, Md.: Robert J. Brady Co., 1982.

Anderson, James W. *Diabetes*. New York: Arco Publishing, 1981.

Born, Dorothy. *Diabetes in the Family*. Bowie, Md.: Robert J. Brady Co., 1982. This book is endorsed by the American Diabetes Association.

Diabetes Forecast, a magazine published bimonthly by the American Diabetes Association, 2 Park Avenue, New York, New York 10016.

Evans, Peter. *Getting On*. London: Granada, 1982.

Jones, Jeanne. *More Calculated Cooking: Practical Recipes for Diabetics and Dieters*. San Francisco: 101 Productions, 1981.

Krall, Leo P. *Joslin Diabetes Manual*, eleventh edition. Philadelphia: Lea & Febiger, 1978.

West, Betty M. *Diabetic Menus, Meals, and Recipes*. New York: Doubleday Publishing Co., 1978.

The address and telephone number of the national headquarters of the American Diabetes Association is:

     2 Park Avenue
     New York, New York 10016
     (212) 683-7444

Index